The Ultimate Cake Cookbook

Dishes, Volume 13

Olivia Bennett

Published by B&H Publishing Group, 2025.

THE ULTIMATE CAKE COOKBOOK

First edition. February 25, 2025.

Copyright © 2025 Olivia Bennett.

ISBN: 979-8230404408

Written by Olivia Bennett.

Table of Contents

To everyone who believes that a slice of cake can brighten any moment—this book is for you.

To my family and friends, who have tasted every experiment (good and bad) with love and patience.

To the bakers, dreamers, and dessert lovers who find joy in the aroma of vanilla, the swirl of frosting, and the first warm bite of a homemade cake.

May your kitchens be filled with sweetness, laughter, and endless celebrations.

Introduction: The Sweet World of Cakes

Cakes are the embodiment of celebration, joy, and indulgence. From marking life's milestones to adding a touch of sweetness to ordinary days, cakes have a timeless appeal that transcends cultures, traditions, and generations. Whether it's a towering layer cake at a wedding, a simple pound cake shared over coffee, or a colorful birthday cake glowing with candles, these baked creations hold a special place in our hearts and kitchens.

This chapter serves as your gateway to the world of cakes, offering insights into their history, their role in everyday life, and the essential tools and techniques needed to create perfect cakes every time. You'll also find tips for overcoming common baking challenges, ensuring that your journey through this book is both enjoyable and successful.

The Timeless Appeal of Cakes

1. A Symbol of Celebration

Cakes have been central to celebrations for centuries. From ancient rituals involving honey-sweetened bread to modern-day confections adorned with intricate decorations, cakes have evolved into a universal symbol of festivity.

- Birthdays: The tradition of birthday cakes dates back to ancient Greece, where round cakes symbolized the moon and were offered to the goddess Artemis.

- Weddings: Elaborate wedding cakes represent prosperity and unity, with origins tracing back to medieval England.

- Festive Holidays: Christmas yule logs, fruitcakes, and New Year's gateaux showcase how cakes can embody the spirit of a season.

2. Everyday Joys

While cakes are often associated with grand occasions, they also bring comfort and delight to everyday life. A slice of warm pound cake with tea or a midweek chocolate cake can turn an ordinary day into something special.

3. A Universal Connection

Every culture has its own take on cakes, from Japanese castella to Italian panettone, reflecting the diversity and creativity of global baking traditions. Cakes connect us across borders, offering a shared language of sweetness.

Essential Tools for Successful Baking

Baking a cake requires precision, patience, and the right tools. Here's a guide to the essentials:

1. Bakeware

- Cake Pans: Invest in round, square, and rectangular pans in various sizes. Non-stick or aluminum pans ensure even baking.

- Springform Pans: Perfect for cheesecakes and delicate bakes that require easy removal.

- Bundt Pans: Used for intricate cakes with decorative shapes.

2. Measuring Tools

- Measuring Cups and Spoons: Accurate measurements are crucial in baking. Use separate sets for dry and liquid ingredients.

- Kitchen Scale: For precision, especially when baking recipes from different regions with varying measurement systems.

3. Mixing Tools

- Mixing Bowls: Have a variety of sizes for different stages of preparation.

- Whisks and Spatulas: Essential for mixing and folding ingredients. Silicone spatulas are particularly versatile.

- Stand Mixer or Hand Mixer: A stand mixer is ideal for heavy batters, while a hand mixer offers convenience for smaller tasks.

4. Specialty Tools

- Offset Spatula: For spreading frosting evenly.

- Bench Scraper: Helps smooth frosting on layer cakes.

- Piping Bags and Tips: For decorating cakes with precision.

- Cake Turntable: Makes frosting and decorating easier and more professional.

Key Ingredients for Baking Success

Understanding your ingredients is fundamental to baking. Each plays a specific role in creating the perfect cake:

1. Flour

- All-Purpose Flour: Suitable for most cakes but can be slightly dense for delicate sponges.

- Cake Flour: Low protein content results in lighter, tender cakes.

- Alternative Flours: Almond, coconut, and gluten-free flours offer options for special diets.

2. Sugar

- Granulated Sugar: Adds sweetness and structure.

- Brown Sugar: Offers moisture and a caramel-like flavor.

- Powdered Sugar: Used for frostings and dusting.

3. Fats

- Butter: Adds flavor and richness. Room temperature butter is key for creaming.

- Oil: Creates moist cakes and works well in recipes like chocolate cake.

- Shortening: Provides stability in frostings.

4. Eggs

- Bind ingredients, add moisture, and provide structure. Room temperature eggs blend better with batters.

5. Leavening Agents

- Baking Powder and Baking Soda: Create lift and lightness. Be sure to use the correct one for your recipe.

- Yeast: For certain cakes like babka or kugelhopf.

6. Liquids

- Milk: Adds moisture and helps create a tender crumb.

- Buttermilk: Provides acidity for a softer texture.

- Water, Coffee, and Juices: Enhance flavor in specific recipes.

7. Flavorings

- Vanilla Extract: A must-have for most cakes.

- Spices: Cinnamon, nutmeg, and cardamom add depth.

- Zests and Extracts: Lemon zest, almond extract, and others customize flavors.

Techniques for Perfect Cakes

1. Prepping the Pan

- Grease and line pans with parchment paper to prevent sticking.

2. Measuring Ingredients

- Always measure accurately. Too much flour can result in dense cakes, while too little can cause collapse.

3. Mixing Batter

- Follow the recipe instructions for mixing times. Overmixing can lead to tough cakes, while undermixing can cause uneven textures.

4. Baking

- Preheat the oven to the correct temperature.

- Use the middle rack for even heat distribution.

- Avoid opening the oven door frequently, which can cause cakes to sink.

5. Cooling

- Allow cakes to cool in the pan for 10–15 minutes before transferring to a wire rack. This prevents breaking or sticking.

Troubleshooting Common Baking Challenges

1. Cake Sinks in the Middle

Cause: Overbeating, underbaking, or too much leavening.

Solution: Measure ingredients accurately, avoid overmixing, and bake fully before opening the oven door.

2. Dry or Crumbly Texture

Cause: Overbaking or too much flour.

Solution: Check your oven temperature with a thermometer and measure flour correctly.

3. Uneven Layers

Cause: Batter not evenly spread or uneven oven racks.

Solution: Rotate pans halfway through baking and level the batter with a spatula.

4. Sticking to the Pan

Cause: Insufficient greasing or cooling.

Solution: Use parchment paper and allow cakes to cool before removing.

5. Frosting Melts or Slides

Cause: Cake not cooled completely or frosting too warm.

Solution: Always frost a fully cooled cake and refrigerate frosting if it becomes too soft.

Conclusion: A Sweet Start

Baking a cake is more than just following a recipe; it's an act of love, creativity, and joy. With the right tools, high-quality ingredients, and careful attention to detail, you can master the art of cake baking and create sweet memories for every occasion.

This introduction sets the stage for your journey through the world of cakes. As you explore the recipes and techniques in this book, remember to embrace the process, experiment with flavors, and, most importantly, enjoy the sweet rewards of your efforts. Happy baking!

Chapter 1: Classic Layer Cakes

Layer cakes are the epitome of celebration, elegance, and indulgence. With their towering presence and rich flavors, they're often the centerpiece of birthdays, weddings, and other special occasions. Whether it's the simplicity of a Classic Vanilla Cake, the decadence of a Rich Chocolate Layer Cake, or the vibrant allure of a Red Velvet Cake, mastering layer cakes opens a world of baking possibilities.

This chapter dives into the fundamentals of crafting perfect layer cakes, shares recipes for three timeless classics, and offers expert tips for achieving even layers and flawless frosting. Whether you're a beginner or a seasoned baker, this guide will elevate your layer cake game.

The Fundamentals of Layer Cakes

1. The Foundation of a Perfect Cake

- Flavors and Textures: A good layer cake should be moist yet sturdy enough to hold its structure. Choose recipes that balance flavor with the ability to support layers and frosting.

- Even Layers: Consistent layers create a visually appealing and stable cake. This is achieved through precise measurements, even baking, and careful assembly.

2. Essential Tools for Layer Cakes

- Cake Pans: Use high-quality, non-stick pans for even baking. Pans with straight sides are ideal for uniform layers.

- Cake Leveler or Serrated Knife: For trimming domed tops and ensuring even layers.

- Cake Turntable: Simplifies the process of frosting and decorating.

- Offset Spatula: A must-have for spreading frosting smoothly.

- Parchment Paper: Prevents cakes from sticking to pans and ensures clean removal.

3. Baking Basics

- Prepping the Pan: Grease the pan, line the bottom with parchment paper, and dust with flour or cocoa powder.

- Room Temperature Ingredients: Allow butter, eggs, and milk to come to room temperature for easier mixing and better texture.

- Measuring Accurately: Weighing ingredients ensures consistent results.

- Preheating the Oven: Always bake in a fully preheated oven to ensure even cooking.

4. Layer Assembly Tips

- Cool cakes completely before assembling.

- Level each layer for stability and aesthetics.

- Use a crumb coat to lock in loose crumbs before applying the final layer of frosting.

Recipe 1: Classic Vanilla Layer Cake

A timeless favorite, the vanilla layer cake serves as a blank canvas for creativity. Its buttery flavor and tender crumb make it perfect for any occasion.

Ingredients:

- 2 1/2 cups (315g) all-purpose flour

- 2 1/2 teaspoons baking powder

- 1/2 teaspoon salt

- 1 cup (227g) unsalted butter, softened

- 2 cups (400g) granulated sugar

- 4 large eggs, room temperature

- 1 tablespoon vanilla extract

- 1 cup (240ml) whole milk, room temperature

Instructions:

1. Preheat oven to 350°F (175°C). Grease and line two 9-inch round cake pans with parchment paper.

2. In a medium bowl, whisk together flour, baking powder, and salt.

3. In a large bowl, beat butter and sugar until light and fluffy, about 3 minutes. Add eggs one at a time, beating well after each addition. Stir in vanilla extract.

4. Add dry ingredients to the butter mixture in three additions, alternating with milk. Begin and end with dry ingredients. Mix until just combined.

5. Divide batter evenly between prepared pans and smooth the tops with a spatula.

6. Bake for 25–30 minutes, or until a toothpick inserted in the center comes out clean.

7. Cool cakes in pans for 10 minutes, then transfer to a wire rack to cool completely.

Tips:

- For added flavor, use vanilla bean paste instead of extract.

- Pair with buttercream or whipped cream frosting for a classic finish.

Recipe 2: Rich Chocolate Layer Cake

This decadent chocolate cake is a must-have for chocoholics. Its deep flavor and moist texture make it an irresistible treat.

Ingredients:

- 1 3/4 cups (220g) all-purpose flour
- 3/4 cup (75g) unsweetened cocoa powder
- 2 teaspoons baking soda
- 1 teaspoon baking powder
- 1/2 teaspoon salt
- 2 cups (400g) granulated sugar
- 1 cup (240ml) buttermilk, room temperature
- 1/2 cup (120ml) vegetable oil
- 2 large eggs, room temperature
- 2 teaspoons vanilla extract
- 1 cup (240ml) hot coffee

Instructions:

1. Preheat oven to 350°F (175°C). Grease and line two 9-inch round cake pans with parchment paper.

2. In a large bowl, sift together flour, cocoa powder, baking soda, baking powder, and salt. Stir in sugar.

3. In a separate bowl, whisk together buttermilk, oil, eggs, and vanilla. Gradually add wet ingredients to the dry ingredients, mixing until smooth. Stir in hot coffee (batter will be thin).

4. Divide batter evenly between prepared pans.

5. Bake for 30–35 minutes, or until a toothpick inserted in the center comes out clean.

6. Cool cakes in pans for 10 minutes, then transfer to a wire rack to cool completely.

Tips:

- Use high-quality cocoa powder for a richer flavor.

- Pair with chocolate ganache or cream cheese frosting for added indulgence.

Recipe 3: Red Velvet Cake

Known for its vibrant color and subtle cocoa flavor, Red Velvet Cake is a Southern classic that's perfect for special occasions.

Ingredients:

- 2 1/2 cups (315g) all-purpose flour
- 2 tablespoons (15g) unsweetened cocoa powder
- 1 teaspoon baking soda
- 1/2 teaspoon salt
- 1/2 cup (120ml) unsalted butter, softened
- 1 1/2 cups (300g) granulated sugar
- 2 large eggs, room temperature
- 1 cup (240ml) buttermilk, room temperature
- 1 tablespoon red food coloring
- 1 teaspoon vanilla extract
- 1 teaspoon white vinegar

Instructions:

1. Preheat oven to 350°F (175°C). Grease and line two 9-inch round cake pans with parchment paper.

2. In a medium bowl, sift together flour, cocoa powder, baking soda, and salt.

3. In a large bowl, beat butter and sugar until light and fluffy. Add eggs one at a time, beating well after each addition.

4. Combine buttermilk, red food coloring, and vanilla. Add dry ingredients to the butter mixture in three additions, alternating with buttermilk mixture. Stir in vinegar.

5. Divide batter evenly between prepared pans.

6. Bake for 25–30 minutes, or until a toothpick inserted in the center comes out clean.

7. Cool cakes in pans for 10 minutes, then transfer to a wire rack to cool completely.

Tips:

- Pair with cream cheese frosting for the classic combination.

- Use gel food coloring for a more vibrant red hue.

Tips for Even Layers and Perfect Frosting

1. Leveling Layers

- Use a cake leveler or serrated knife to trim domed tops.

- Freeze cake layers for 15 minutes before trimming for easier handling.

2. Crumb Coat

- Apply a thin layer of frosting to seal in crumbs. Refrigerate for 15–30 minutes before applying the final layer.

3. Frosting Techniques

- Use an offset spatula for smooth application.

- Use a bench scraper to achieve sharp edges.

4. Decorating

- Pipe rosettes, swirls, or borders for added flair.

- Garnish with fresh fruit, sprinkles, or edible flowers for a polished finish.

Conclusion

Mastering classic layer cakes like Vanilla, Chocolate, and Red Velvet is a rewarding skill that unlocks endless possibilities in baking. With the right techniques and a touch of creativity, these recipes can serve as a foundation for crafting cakes that impress both visually and in flavor. Let this chapter inspire you to embrace the art of layer cakes and create sweet memories for every occasion.

Chapter 2: Crowd-Pleasing Sheet Cakes

Sheet cakes are the unsung heroes of large gatherings. They are easy to make, serve, and customize, making them a go-to option for everything from birthday parties to potlucks and casual family dinners. Despite their simplicity, sheet cakes can deliver the same level of flavor and presentation as more elaborate cake styles, with minimal effort. In this chapter, we'll explore the charm of sheet cakes, present recipes for classics like Texas Sheet Cake, Lemon Poppy Seed Cake, and Carrot Sheet Cake, and share tips for decorating them to suit both casual and formal occasions.

The Appeal of Sheet Cakes

1. Perfect for Feeding a Crowd
    - Sheet cakes are baked in a single pan, making them easy to portion and serve.
    - They can accommodate a wide range of flavors and decorations to suit any occasion.
    2. Easy to Transport
    - Whether you're attending a potluck, school event, or office party, sheet cakes are ideal for transporting without worrying about layers shifting or collapsing.
    3. Customizable
    - From simple icing and sprinkles to intricate piping and edible decorations, sheet cakes offer endless opportunities for creativity.
    4. Time-Saving
    - Sheet cakes require less assembly and decoration time compared to layered cakes, making them an excellent choice for busy schedules.

Essential Tools for Sheet Cake Success

1. Sheet Pans
    - Use a high-quality, heavy-duty sheet pan to ensure even baking. Common sizes include:
    - Quarter Sheet (9x13 inches): Serves about 12–15 people.

- Half Sheet (12x18 inches): Serves 24–36 people.

2. Parchment Paper

- Line the bottom of the pan with parchment paper for easy removal and cleanup.

3. Cooling Racks

- Allow cakes to cool completely on a wire rack before frosting to prevent melting or sliding.

4. Spatulas and Piping Bags

- Use offset spatulas for spreading frosting and piping bags with various tips for decorative elements.

Recipe 1: Texas Sheet Cake

A Southern classic, Texas Sheet Cake is beloved for its rich, fudgy flavor and melt-in-your-mouth texture. Its thin layer of chocolate cake is topped with a glossy chocolate frosting and chopped pecans for a decadent treat.

Ingredients for the Cake:

- 2 cups (250g) all-purpose flour
- 2 cups (400g) granulated sugar
- 1/4 teaspoon salt
- 1 teaspoon baking soda
- 1/2 cup (120ml) unsalted butter
- 1/2 cup (120ml) vegetable oil
- 1/4 cup (25g) unsweetened cocoa powder
- 1 cup (240ml) water
- 1/2 cup (120ml) buttermilk
- 2 large eggs
- 1 teaspoon vanilla extract

Ingredients for the Frosting:

- 1/2 cup (120ml) unsalted butter
- 1/4 cup (25g) unsweetened cocoa powder
- 1/4 cup (60ml) milk
- 3 cups (375g) powdered sugar
- 1 teaspoon vanilla extract
- 1/2 cup (60g) chopped pecans

Instructions:

1. Preheat oven to 350°F (175°C). Grease and line a 9x13-inch sheet pan with parchment paper.

2. In a large bowl, whisk together flour, sugar, salt, and baking soda.

3. In a medium saucepan, melt butter and oil over medium heat. Stir in cocoa powder and water, bringing to a boil. Remove from heat and pour into the dry ingredients, mixing until smooth.

4. In a separate bowl, whisk together buttermilk, eggs, and vanilla. Stir into the batter until combined.

5. Pour the batter into the prepared pan and bake for 25–30 minutes, or until a toothpick inserted in the center comes out clean.

6. For the frosting, melt butter in a saucepan over medium heat. Stir in cocoa powder and milk, bringing to a simmer. Remove from heat and whisk in powdered sugar and vanilla until smooth.

7. Pour the warm frosting over the warm cake, spreading evenly. Sprinkle with chopped pecans. Let cool completely before slicing.

Tips:

- Substitute walnuts or omit nuts if desired.

- For added depth, use brewed coffee instead of water in the batter.

Recipe 2: Lemon Poppy Seed Cake

This bright and zesty sheet cake is a refreshing option for spring and summer gatherings. The poppy seeds add a delightful crunch, while the lemon glaze enhances the citrus flavor.

Ingredients for the Cake:

- 2 1/2 cups (315g) all-purpose flour
- 2 teaspoons baking powder
- 1/2 teaspoon baking soda
- 1/4 teaspoon salt
- 1/2 cup (120ml) unsalted butter, softened
- 1/2 cup (120ml) vegetable oil
- 1 3/4 cups (350g) granulated sugar
- 4 large eggs
- 1 tablespoon lemon zest

- 1/2 cup (120ml) lemon juice
- 1 cup (240ml) buttermilk
- 2 tablespoons poppy seeds
Ingredients for the Glaze:
- 1 cup (125g) powdered sugar
- 2–3 tablespoons lemon juice
Instructions:

1. Preheat oven to 350°F (175°C). Grease and line a 9x13-inch sheet pan with parchment paper.

2. In a medium bowl, whisk together flour, baking powder, baking soda, and salt.

3. In a large bowl, beat butter, oil, and sugar until light and fluffy. Add eggs one at a time, mixing well after each addition. Stir in lemon zest and juice.

4. Add dry ingredients to the wet ingredients in three additions, alternating with buttermilk. Stir in poppy seeds.

5. Pour batter into the prepared pan and bake for 30–35 minutes, or until a toothpick inserted in the center comes out clean.

6. For the glaze, whisk together powdered sugar and lemon juice until smooth. Drizzle over the cooled cake.

Tips:
- Add a layer of cream cheese frosting for a richer option.
- Garnish with candied lemon slices or edible flowers for a stunning presentation.

Recipe 3: Carrot Sheet Cake

Packed with shredded carrots, warm spices, and a luscious cream cheese frosting, this sheet cake is a crowd-pleaser for any occasion.

Ingredients for the Cake:
- 2 cups (250g) all-purpose flour
- 2 teaspoons baking powder
- 1/2 teaspoon baking soda
- 1 teaspoon cinnamon
- 1/2 teaspoon nutmeg
- 1/4 teaspoon salt

- 1/2 cup (120ml) vegetable oil
- 1/2 cup (120ml) unsweetened applesauce
- 1 1/2 cups (300g) granulated sugar
- 3 large eggs
- 2 teaspoons vanilla extract
- 2 cups (250g) grated carrots
- 1/2 cup (60g) chopped walnuts or pecans (optional)

Ingredients for the Frosting:
- 8 oz (225g) cream cheese, softened
- 1/2 cup (120g) unsalted butter, softened
- 3 cups (375g) powdered sugar
- 1 teaspoon vanilla extract

Instructions:

1. Preheat oven to 350°F (175°C). Grease and line a 9x13-inch sheet pan with parchment paper.

2. In a medium bowl, whisk together flour, baking powder, baking soda, cinnamon, nutmeg, and salt.

3. In a large bowl, beat oil, applesauce, sugar, eggs, and vanilla until smooth. Gradually add dry ingredients, mixing until combined. Fold in grated carrots and nuts.

4. Pour batter into the prepared pan and bake for 30–35 minutes, or until a toothpick inserted in the center comes out clean.

5. For the frosting, beat cream cheese and butter until creamy. Gradually add powdered sugar and vanilla, beating until smooth. Spread over the cooled cake.

Tips:
- Sprinkle with toasted coconut or chopped nuts for extra texture.
- Substitute pineapple for applesauce for a tropical twist.

Decorating Ideas for Any Occasion

1. Casual Gatherings
   - Rustic Look: Spread frosting with an offset spatula for a natural, unpolished look.
   - Simple Garnishes: Top with sprinkles, chopped nuts, or fresh fruit.

2. Formal Occasions

- Piping: Use piping bags to create borders, flowers, or decorative swirls.

- Themed Toppings: Add edible glitter, gold leaf, or fondant decorations to match the event theme.

3. Personalization

- Use stencils and powdered sugar or cocoa powder to create designs.

- Write messages with colored frosting or melted chocolate.

Conclusion

Sheet cakes are the perfect blend of simplicity and elegance, making them a versatile choice for gatherings of any size. Recipes like Texas Sheet Cake, Lemon Poppy Seed Cake, and Carrot Sheet Cake showcase the variety and charm of these easy-to-make desserts. With creative decorations and thoughtful touches, sheet cakes can steal the spotlight at both casual and formal events. Let this chapter inspire you to embrace the ease and beauty of sheet cakes, ensuring your next gathering is both memorable and delicious.

Chapter 3: Bundt and Pound Cakes

Bundt and pound cakes are timeless classics in the world of baking. Known for their simplicity, rich flavors, and versatility, these cakes are ideal for everything from casual coffee breaks to elegant celebrations. Their dense texture and decorative designs make them stand out, yet they remain approachable for bakers of all skill levels. This chapter dives deep into the charm of Bundt and pound cakes, featuring recipes for Classic Lemon Pound Cake, Marble Bundt Cake, and Cream Cheese Pound Cake. Additionally, it offers practical tips for achieving the perfect texture and ensuring cakes don't stick to the pan.

The Allure of Bundt and Pound Cakes

1. The History of Pound Cakes

- The pound cake originated in Europe in the early 18th century, named for its simple recipe: a pound each of butter, sugar, eggs, and flour.

- Over time, variations introduced lighter textures, flavored extracts, and additional ingredients like cream cheese or fruit.

2. The Rise of Bundt Cakes

- Bundt cakes gained popularity in the mid-20th century thanks to the iconic Bundt pan, introduced by Nordic Ware. Its fluted design ensures even baking and creates visually stunning cakes.

3. Why We Love Them

- Simplicity: Minimal decoration is needed; the pan design often doubles as the presentation.

- Versatility: These cakes can be flavored with citrus, chocolate, nuts, or spices and paired with glazes, syrups, or powdered sugar.

- Longevity: Dense textures ensure they stay moist for days, making them perfect for gifting or make-ahead baking.

Essential Tools and Techniques

1. The Perfect Pan

- Material: Opt for heavy-duty aluminum or cast-iron Bundt pans for even heat distribution.

- Size: Most recipes are designed for 10- or 12-cup pans. Adjust baking times if using a smaller or larger pan.

2. Preparing the Pan

- Greasing: Use a pastry brush to coat the pan with melted butter or non-stick spray, ensuring you reach every crevice.

- Flouring: Dust the greased pan with flour (or cocoa powder for chocolate cakes) and tap out excess. This step prevents sticking.

3. Mixing Tips

- Creaming Butter and Sugar: Beat until light and fluffy to incorporate air for a better crumb.

- Room Temperature Ingredients: Ensure butter, eggs, and dairy are at room temperature for easier mixing.

- Avoid Overmixing: Overworking the batter can result in dense cakes. Mix until just combined.

4. Baking Essentials

- Low and Slow: Bundt and pound cakes often require lower oven temperatures (325–350°F) and longer baking times.

- Test for Doneness: Insert a skewer or toothpick into the center; it should come out clean or with a few moist crumbs.

5. Cooling and Releasing

- Cooling: Allow the cake to cool in the pan for 10–15 minutes before inverting it onto a wire rack.

- Releasing the Cake: Gently tap the pan and loosen edges with a knife if necessary. If the cake resists, place a damp towel over the inverted pan for a few minutes to loosen it.

Recipe 1: Classic Lemon Pound Cake

This Lemon Pound Cake is a delightful blend of buttery richness and zesty brightness, perfect for any occasion. A lemon glaze adds an extra burst of citrus flavor.

Ingredients:

- 2 1/2 cups (315g) all-purpose flour
- 1/2 teaspoon baking powder
- 1/4 teaspoon salt

- 1 cup (227g) unsalted butter, softened
- 2 cups (400g) granulated sugar
- 4 large eggs, room temperature
- 1/3 cup (80ml) lemon juice
- 1 tablespoon lemon zest
- 1 teaspoon vanilla extract
- 1/2 cup (120ml) buttermilk, room temperature

For the Glaze:
- 1 cup (125g) powdered sugar
- 2–3 tablespoons lemon juice

Instructions:

1. Preheat oven to 325°F (165°C). Grease and flour a 10-cup Bundt pan.

2. In a medium bowl, whisk together flour, baking powder, and salt.

3. In a large bowl, cream butter and sugar until light and fluffy, about 3 minutes. Add eggs one at a time, mixing well after each addition. Stir in lemon juice, zest, and vanilla.

4. Gradually add dry ingredients to the butter mixture, alternating with buttermilk. Begin and end with the dry ingredients. Mix until just combined.

5. Pour batter into the prepared pan and smooth the top. Bake for 55–65 minutes, or until a toothpick inserted in the center comes out clean.

6. Cool in the pan for 10 minutes before inverting onto a wire rack.

7. For the glaze, whisk powdered sugar and lemon juice until smooth. Drizzle over the cooled cake.

Tips:
- Substitute lime or orange zest for a different citrus flavor.
- Add poppy seeds to the batter for added texture.

Recipe 2: Marble Bundt Cake

This Marble Bundt Cake combines rich chocolate and vanilla batters for a stunning swirl effect. It's as beautiful as it is delicious.

Ingredients:
- 2 1/4 cups (280g) all-purpose flour
- 2 teaspoons baking powder

- 1/2 teaspoon salt
- 1 cup (227g) unsalted butter, softened
- 2 cups (400g) granulated sugar
- 4 large eggs, room temperature
- 1 teaspoon vanilla extract
- 1 cup (240ml) whole milk, room temperature
- 1/4 cup (25g) unsweetened cocoa powder
- 2 tablespoons hot water

Instructions:

1. Preheat oven to 350°F (175°C). Grease and flour a 12-cup Bundt pan.

2. In a medium bowl, whisk together flour, baking powder, and salt.

3. In a large bowl, cream butter and sugar until light and fluffy. Add eggs one at a time, mixing well after each addition. Stir in vanilla.

4. Gradually add dry ingredients to the butter mixture, alternating with milk. Mix until just combined.

5. Remove 1/3 of the batter and place it in a separate bowl. Stir in cocoa powder and hot water until smooth.

6. Pour half the vanilla batter into the prepared pan, followed by the chocolate batter. Top with the remaining vanilla batter. Swirl the batters gently with a knife to create a marbled effect.

7. Bake for 50–60 minutes, or until a toothpick inserted in the center comes out clean. Cool in the pan for 10 minutes before inverting onto a wire rack.

Tips:

- Dust with powdered sugar or drizzle with chocolate glaze for a polished finish.

- Add a teaspoon of instant coffee to the chocolate batter for enhanced depth.

Recipe 3: Cream Cheese Pound Cake

This Cream Cheese Pound Cake is incredibly moist and rich, with a slight tang from the cream cheese. It's a classic dessert that needs no embellishment.

Ingredients:
- 3 cups (375g) all-purpose flour
- 1/2 teaspoon baking powder
- 1/2 teaspoon salt
- 1 1/2 cups (340g) unsalted butter, softened
- 8 oz (225g) cream cheese, softened
- 3 cups (600g) granulated sugar
- 6 large eggs, room temperature
- 1 teaspoon vanilla extract

Instructions:

1. Preheat oven to 325°F (165°C). Grease and flour a 10-cup Bundt pan.

2. In a medium bowl, whisk together flour, baking powder, and salt.

3. In a large bowl, cream butter, cream cheese, and sugar until light and fluffy, about 5 minutes. Add eggs one at a time, mixing well after each addition. Stir in vanilla.

4. Gradually add dry ingredients to the butter mixture, mixing until just combined.

5. Pour batter into the prepared pan and smooth the top. Bake for 70–80 minutes, or until a toothpick inserted in the center comes out clean.

6. Cool in the pan for 15 minutes before inverting onto a wire rack.

Tips:
- Serve with fresh berries or a dollop of whipped cream for added elegance.
- Replace vanilla extract with almond extract for a unique twist.

Conclusion

Bundt and pound cakes are celebrated for their simplicity, versatility, and stunning presentation. Recipes like Classic Lemon Pound Cake, Marble Bundt Cake, and Cream Cheese Pound Cake showcase the range of flavors and styles you can achieve with these timeless bakes. By following the tips for preparation, mixing, and baking, you'll consistently create cakes that are as visually impressive as they are delicious. Let this chapter inspire you to explore the world of Bundt and pound cakes, ensuring every bake is a show-stopping success.

Chapter 4: Cheesecakes

Cheesecake is one of the most luxurious and indulgent desserts, beloved for its creamy texture and versatility. Whether you're crafting a dense New York-style cheesecake, swirling in rich chocolate, or assembling a light, no-bake berry version, mastering the art of cheesecake opens a world of delectable possibilities. While cheesecakes may seem intimidating to make, with the right techniques and a bit of patience, you can achieve smooth, crack-free perfection every time.

This chapter delves into the essentials of cheesecake-making, offering detailed guidance on techniques like using water baths, avoiding cracks, and achieving the perfect consistency. It also provides recipes for three iconic variations: New York Cheesecake, Chocolate Swirl Cheesecake, and No-Bake Berry Cheesecake.

The Art of a Perfect Cheesecake

1. Understanding the Basics

A cheesecake is a harmonious blend of cream cheese, sugar, eggs, and other ingredients, baked (or chilled) into a luscious dessert. Its success relies on achieving a balance between smooth texture, rich flavor, and an attractive appearance.

2. The Anatomy of a Cheesecake

- The Crust: Often made from crushed graham crackers, cookies, or biscuits mixed with butter, providing a crunchy contrast to the creamy filling.

- The Filling: A mixture of cream cheese, sugar, and eggs, often flavored with vanilla, chocolate, fruit, or spices.

- The Topping (Optional): A final layer, such as sour cream, fruit compote, or ganache, to enhance flavor and presentation.

3. Types of Cheesecakes

- Baked Cheesecakes: Dense and rich, requiring precise baking techniques.

- No-Bake Cheesecakes: Lighter and simpler, set in the refrigerator with gelatin or whipped cream.

Techniques for Smooth, Crack-Free Cheesecakes

1. Room Temperature Ingredients

- Ensure cream cheese, eggs, and other dairy ingredients are at room temperature to blend smoothly without lumps.

2. Avoid Overmixing

- Overmixing incorporates excess air into the batter, which can cause cracking during baking. Mix just until combined.

3. Use a Water Bath (Bain-Marie)

- A water bath provides gentle, even heat, reducing the risk of cracks.

- How to Set It Up:

1. Wrap the bottom of the springform pan in heavy-duty aluminum foil to prevent leaks.

2. Place the pan in a larger roasting pan.

3. Pour hot water into the roasting pan until it reaches halfway up the sides of the cheesecake pan.

4. Bake Low and Slow

- Bake at a low temperature (typically 300–325°F) to ensure even cooking and a creamy texture.

5. Don't Overbake

- The center of the cheesecake should jiggle slightly when done. It will firm up as it cools.

6. Gradual Cooling

- Cool the cheesecake in the oven with the door slightly ajar for 1 hour to prevent sudden temperature changes, which can cause cracking.

7. Refrigeration

- Chill the cheesecake for at least 4–6 hours, preferably overnight, for optimal flavor and texture.

Recipe 1: New York Cheesecake

A quintessential classic, New York Cheesecake is dense, creamy, and subtly tangy, with a graham cracker crust and a luxurious cream cheese filling.

Ingredients for the Crust:

- 2 cups (200g) graham cracker crumbs

- 1/4 cup (50g) granulated sugar

- 1/2 cup (120g) unsalted butter, melted

Ingredients for the Filling:

- 4 (8 oz/225g each) packages cream cheese, softened
- 1 1/4 cups (250g) granulated sugar
- 1 cup (240g) sour cream, room temperature
- 2 teaspoons vanilla extract
- 4 large eggs, room temperature

Instructions:

1. Preheat oven to 325°F (165°C). Grease a 9-inch springform pan.

2. Combine graham cracker crumbs, sugar, and melted butter. Press evenly into the bottom of the prepared pan. Bake for 10 minutes and set aside to cool.

3. In a large bowl, beat cream cheese and sugar until smooth. Add sour cream and vanilla, mixing until combined.

4. Add eggs one at a time, mixing on low speed until just incorporated. Avoid overmixing.

5. Pour the filling over the crust. Wrap the bottom of the pan in aluminum foil and place it in a roasting pan. Add hot water to the roasting pan to create a water bath.

6. Bake for 1 hour and 15 minutes, or until the edges are set but the center jiggles slightly.

7. Turn off the oven and let the cheesecake cool inside with the door ajar for 1 hour. Refrigerate for at least 6 hours or overnight before serving.

Tips:

- Serve with a dollop of whipped cream or fresh berries for added flavor.
- Add a teaspoon of lemon zest for a citrusy twist.

Recipe 2: Chocolate Swirl Cheesecake

This decadent cheesecake combines a creamy vanilla base with rich chocolate swirls, creating a dessert that's as stunning as it is delicious.

Ingredients for the Crust:

- 2 cups (200g) chocolate cookie crumbs
- 1/4 cup (50g) granulated sugar
- 1/2 cup (120g) unsalted butter, melted

Ingredients for the Filling:

- 3 (8 oz/225g each) packages cream cheese, softened
- 1 cup (200g) granulated sugar
- 1 cup (240g) sour cream, room temperature
- 3 large eggs, room temperature
- 2 teaspoons vanilla extract
- 4 oz (115g) semi-sweet chocolate, melted and slightly cooled

Instructions:

1. Preheat oven to 325°F (165°C). Grease a 9-inch springform pan.

2. Mix cookie crumbs, sugar, and melted butter. Press into the bottom of the pan and bake for 10 minutes. Cool completely.

3. In a large bowl, beat cream cheese and sugar until smooth. Add sour cream and vanilla, mixing well.

4. Add eggs one at a time, mixing on low speed until combined.

5. Remove 1 cup of batter and mix with melted chocolate. Pour the vanilla batter into the crust. Drop spoonfuls of chocolate batter on top and use a knife to swirl it into the vanilla batter.

6. Bake in a water bath for 1 hour, or until the edges are set and the center jiggles slightly. Cool and chill as directed in the New York Cheesecake recipe.

Tips:

- Substitute white chocolate or dark chocolate for the semi-sweet chocolate.

- Garnish with chocolate shavings or whipped cream.

Recipe 3: No-Bake Berry Cheesecake

Light, refreshing, and easy to prepare, this no-bake cheesecake features a creamy filling topped with a vibrant berry compote.

Ingredients for the Crust:

- 2 cups (200g) digestive biscuit or graham cracker crumbs
- 1/4 cup (50g) granulated sugar
- 1/2 cup (120g) unsalted butter, melted

Ingredients for the Filling:

- 16 oz (450g) cream cheese, softened
- 1 cup (240g) heavy cream, whipped to stiff peaks
- 1/2 cup (100g) granulated sugar

- 1 teaspoon vanilla extract

Ingredients for the Berry Topping:

- 2 cups (300g) mixed berries (strawberries, raspberries, blueberries)
- 1/4 cup (50g) granulated sugar
- 1 tablespoon lemon juice

Instructions:

1. Combine crust ingredients and press into the bottom of a 9-inch springform pan. Chill for 15 minutes.

2. Beat cream cheese, sugar, and vanilla until smooth. Fold in whipped cream until combined. Spread the filling evenly over the crust. Chill for at least 4 hours or until set.

3. For the topping, combine berries, sugar, and lemon juice in a saucepan. Cook over medium heat until the berries soften and the mixture thickens slightly. Cool completely before spreading over the cheesecake.

Tips:

- Use gelatin or agar-agar in the filling for extra stability.
- Swap berries for other fruits like mango, passion fruit, or cherries.

Conclusion

Cheesecakes are a true testament to the art of baking, offering endless opportunities for creativity and indulgence. Recipes like New York Cheesecake, Chocolate Swirl Cheesecake, and No-Bake Berry Cheesecake showcase the variety and versatility of this beloved dessert. With the techniques and tips outlined in this chapter, you'll be well-equipped to create smooth, crack-free cheesecakes that are as visually stunning as they are delicious. Let your imagination guide you as you explore flavors, textures, and toppings to craft cheesecakes that leave a lasting impression.

Chapter 5: Cupcakes and Mini Cakes

Cupcakes and mini cakes are the perfect bite-sized indulgence, offering the joy of cake in a convenient, individual format. These little desserts are versatile, making them ideal for everything from birthday parties to weddings, and they allow for endless creativity in flavors and decoration. Whether you're baking classic cupcakes with a twist or elegant mini cakes for a sophisticated event, these small treats can pack big flavor.

This chapter explores the art of crafting flawless cupcakes and mini cakes, with recipes for Chocolate Ganache Cupcakes, Vanilla Bean Cupcakes, and Mini Fruit Tarts. You'll also find inspiration for decorating, flavor combinations, and presentation ideas to elevate your creations.

The Appeal of Cupcakes and Mini Cakes

1. Individual Portions
    - Perfectly portioned, these cakes are easy to serve and enjoy without the need for slicing or additional utensils.
    2. Versatility
    - Cupcakes and mini cakes are adaptable to any theme, flavor, or occasion, from casual gatherings to formal events.
    3. Creative Freedom
    - Their small size encourages experimentation with flavors, fillings, and decorations.
    4. Easy Storage and Transport
    - Cupcakes and mini cakes are simpler to store and transport compared to full-sized cakes, making them ideal for on-the-go events.

Essential Tools for Success

1. Baking Equipment
    - Cupcake Pans: Use standard or mini muffin pans for cupcakes. Specialty molds can create unique shapes.
    - Mini Cake Pans: Look for 4-inch round or square pans for individual cakes.

- Paper Liners: Cupcake liners ensure easy removal and add a decorative touch.

2. Decorating Tools

- Piping Bags and Tips: Use a variety of tips for intricate designs.

- Offset Spatula: Perfect for spreading frosting evenly on mini cakes.

- Fondant Tools: Ideal for creating detailed decorations.

3. Presentation Supplies

- Cupcake Stands: Showcase cupcakes at parties or events.

- Boxes and Wrappers: For gifting or transporting cupcakes and mini cakes.

Tips for Perfect Cupcakes and Mini Cakes

1. Mixing the Batter

- Avoid overmixing to prevent dense or tough cakes. Mix just until the ingredients are combined.

- Use room temperature ingredients for a smoother batter.

2. Portioning Batter

- Use an ice cream scoop or piping bag for consistent cupcake sizes. This ensures even baking.

3. Baking

- Preheat the oven fully to avoid uneven baking.

- Rotate pans halfway through baking to ensure even heat distribution.

4. Cooling

- Allow cupcakes and mini cakes to cool completely before decorating to prevent frosting from melting.

Recipe 1: Chocolate Ganache Cupcakes

These indulgent cupcakes feature a rich chocolate base topped with silky ganache, making them a showstopper for any chocolate lover.

Ingredients for the Cupcakes:

- 1 1/2 cups (190g) all-purpose flour

- 1/2 cup (50g) unsweetened cocoa powder

- 1 teaspoon baking powder

- 1/2 teaspoon baking soda

- 1/4 teaspoon salt

- 1/2 cup (120ml) vegetable oil
- 1 cup (200g) granulated sugar
- 2 large eggs, room temperature
- 1 teaspoon vanilla extract
- 1/2 cup (120ml) buttermilk, room temperature
- 1/2 cup (120ml) hot coffee

Ingredients for the Ganache:
- 8 oz (225g) semi-sweet chocolate, finely chopped
- 1/2 cup (120ml) heavy cream
- 1 tablespoon butter, softened

Instructions:

1. Preheat oven to 350°F (175°C). Line a 12-cup muffin pan with paper liners.

2. In a medium bowl, sift together flour, cocoa powder, baking powder, baking soda, and salt.

3. In a large bowl, whisk together oil and sugar. Add eggs and vanilla, mixing until smooth.

4. Gradually add dry ingredients, alternating with buttermilk. Stir in hot coffee until the batter is smooth (it will be thin).

5. Divide batter evenly among cupcake liners, filling each about two-thirds full. Bake for 18–20 minutes, or until a toothpick inserted in the center comes out clean. Cool completely.

6. For the ganache, heat cream until just simmering. Pour over chopped chocolate and let sit for 2 minutes. Stir until smooth, then mix in butter. Let cool slightly before spreading or piping onto cupcakes.

Tips:
- Garnish with chocolate shavings, berries, or a sprinkle of sea salt for extra flair.
- Use dark chocolate for a more intense flavor.

Recipe 2: Vanilla Bean Cupcakes

These classic cupcakes are infused with vanilla bean for a fragrant and flavorful treat, perfect for pairing with various frostings and fillings.

Ingredients:

- 1 1/2 cups (190g) all-purpose flour
- 1 1/2 teaspoons baking powder
- 1/4 teaspoon salt
- 1/2 cup (115g) unsalted butter, softened
- 1 cup (200g) granulated sugar
- 2 large eggs, room temperature
- 1 teaspoon vanilla bean paste (or extract)
- 1/2 cup (120ml) whole milk, room temperature

Ingredients for the Frosting:
- 1 cup (230g) unsalted butter, softened
- 3 cups (375g) powdered sugar
- 2 tablespoons heavy cream
- 1 teaspoon vanilla bean paste

Instructions:

1. Preheat oven to 350°F (175°C). Line a 12-cup muffin pan with paper liners.

2. In a medium bowl, whisk together flour, baking powder, and salt.

3. In a large bowl, beat butter and sugar until light and fluffy. Add eggs one at a time, then mix in vanilla bean paste.

4. Add dry ingredients to the wet mixture in three additions, alternating with milk. Mix until smooth.

5. Divide batter evenly among cupcake liners. Bake for 18–20 minutes, or until a toothpick inserted in the center comes out clean. Cool completely.

6. For the frosting, beat butter until creamy. Gradually add powdered sugar, alternating with heavy cream. Mix in vanilla bean paste. Pipe or spread onto cooled cupcakes.

Tips:
- Fill cupcakes with jam or custard for a surprise center.
- Decorate with sprinkles, edible flowers, or fondant shapes.

Recipe 3: Mini Fruit Tarts

These elegant mini cakes feature a buttery tart shell filled with creamy custard and topped with fresh fruit, making them perfect for sophisticated events.

Ingredients for the Tart Shells:

- 1 1/4 cups (155g) all-purpose flour
- 1/4 cup (50g) granulated sugar
- 1/2 cup (115g) unsalted butter, cold and cubed
- 1 large egg yolk
- 2 tablespoons cold water

Ingredients for the Filling:
- 2 cups (480ml) whole milk
- 1/2 cup (100g) granulated sugar
- 1/4 cup (30g) cornstarch
- 4 large egg yolks
- 1 teaspoon vanilla extract

Toppings:
- Assorted fresh fruits (berries, kiwi, mango, etc.)
- Apricot glaze (optional)

Instructions:

1. For the shells, combine flour and sugar in a food processor. Add butter and pulse until the mixture resembles coarse crumbs. Add egg yolk and cold water, pulsing until the dough comes together.

2. Wrap dough in plastic wrap and refrigerate for 30 minutes. Roll out and cut into circles to fit mini tart pans. Press dough into pans and prick the bottoms with a fork. Bake at 350°F (175°C) for 10–12 minutes, or until golden. Cool completely.

3. For the filling, heat milk in a saucepan until just simmering. In a bowl, whisk sugar, cornstarch, and egg yolks. Gradually add hot milk to the egg mixture, whisking constantly. Return to the saucepan and cook until thickened. Remove from heat and stir in vanilla. Cool before using.

4. Fill tart shells with custard and top with fresh fruit. Brush with apricot glaze if desired.

Tips:
- Use pre-made tart shells for a time-saving option.
- Experiment with flavored custards, such as chocolate or citrus.

Creative Decorating Ideas

1. Elegant Finishes

- Pipe rosettes or swirls of frosting for a professional look.

- Dust cupcakes with edible glitter or gold leaf for a luxurious touch.

2. Themed Designs

- Match decorations to holidays or events, such as pastel frosting for Easter or red and green sprinkles for Christmas.

- Use fondant to create themed shapes, like flowers, animals, or seasonal symbols.

3. Fun for Kids

- Top cupcakes with colorful sprinkles, candy, or mini cookies.

- Create interactive designs, like adding a candy-filled center that spills out when bitten.

4. Presentation Matters

- Arrange cupcakes in patterns, such as flowers or hearts, for a striking centerpiece.

- Serve mini cakes on individual plates with complementary garnishes.

Conclusion

Cupcakes and mini cakes are the perfect combination of simplicity and sophistication, offering endless opportunities for flavor and design. Recipes like Chocolate Ganache Cupcakes, Vanilla Bean Cupcakes, and Mini Fruit Tarts showcase the versatility and charm of these small treats. With a few essential tools, creative ideas, and the tips provided in this chapter, you can craft impressive, crowd-pleasing desserts for any occasion. Whether you're baking for a casual get-together or an elegant celebration, let your imagination guide you as you create these delightful individual cakes.

Chapter 6: Gluten-Free Cakes

Gluten-free baking has become an essential part of modern cooking, whether due to dietary restrictions, health benefits, or simply exploring new culinary possibilities. Gluten-free cakes are no exception, offering the same delicious textures and flavors without relying on traditional wheat flour. However, baking without gluten presents unique challenges, requiring creativity and an understanding of alternative flours and techniques.

This chapter is a comprehensive guide to crafting delicious, gluten-free cakes, featuring recipes for Flourless Chocolate Cake, Almond Lemon Cake, and Gluten-Free Carrot Cake. We'll also delve into essential tips for working with alternative flours like almond and coconut flour to achieve exceptional results every time.

Understanding Gluten-Free Baking

1. What is Gluten?

Gluten is a protein found in wheat, barley, and rye. It provides structure and elasticity in baked goods, helping cakes rise and maintain their shape.

2. The Challenge of Gluten-Free Baking

Without gluten, cakes can become crumbly, dense, or dry if not handled properly. Achieving the right balance of moisture, structure, and flavor requires careful ingredient selection and preparation.

3. Benefits of Gluten-Free Cakes

- Inclusivity: Perfect for those with celiac disease, gluten intolerance, or wheat allergies.

- Versatility: Alternative flours offer unique flavors and nutritional benefits.

- Health: Many gluten-free cakes use whole foods and are naturally lower in processed ingredients.

Essential Tips for Gluten-Free Baking

1. Choose the Right Flour Alternatives

- Almond Flour: Adds moisture and a nutty flavor; ideal for dense cakes like pound cakes.

- Coconut Flour: Highly absorbent, requiring additional liquid or eggs; best for sponge cakes.

- Gluten-Free All-Purpose Flour: Pre-blended mixtures mimic traditional flour and are suitable for most recipes.

- Rice Flour: Creates light and tender textures but can be gritty if not paired with other flours.

2. Use Binding Agents

Without gluten, cakes need alternative binders to hold their structure.

- Eggs: Provide structure and moisture.

- Xanthan Gum or Guar Gum: Small amounts (1/4 teaspoon per cup of flour) improve elasticity.

- Flaxseed or Chia Seeds: Mixed with water, these create a gel-like consistency that acts as a binder.

3. Add Moisture

Gluten-free cakes can dry out quickly. Use ingredients like yogurt, sour cream, applesauce, or mashed bananas to retain moisture.

4. Blend Flours

Using a combination of flours, such as almond and coconut, balances flavor and texture for a more satisfying cake.

5. Don't Overmix

Gluten-free batters don't need excessive mixing. Overmixing can lead to dense, gummy cakes. Mix until just combined.

Recipe 1: Flourless Chocolate Cake

Rich, decadent, and naturally gluten-free, this Flourless Chocolate Cake is a timeless dessert perfect for special occasions.

Ingredients:
- 8 oz (225g) dark chocolate, chopped
- 1/2 cup (115g) unsalted butter
- 3/4 cup (150g) granulated sugar
- 4 large eggs, separated
- 1/4 teaspoon salt

- 1 teaspoon vanilla extract
- 1/4 cup (25g) unsweetened cocoa powder

Instructions:

1. Preheat oven to 350°F (175°C). Grease a 9-inch springform pan and line the bottom with parchment paper.

2. In a heatproof bowl, melt chocolate and butter over a double boiler or in the microwave, stirring until smooth. Let cool slightly.

3. Stir in sugar, egg yolks, vanilla, and cocoa powder until well combined.

4. In a separate bowl, beat egg whites and salt until stiff peaks form. Gently fold the egg whites into the chocolate mixture in three additions.

5. Pour batter into the prepared pan and smooth the top. Bake for 25–30 minutes, or until the center is set but still slightly soft.

6. Cool completely before removing from the pan. Dust with powdered sugar or cocoa powder before serving.

Tips:

- Serve with whipped cream or a berry compote for contrast.
- Use high-quality chocolate for the best flavor.

Recipe 2: Almond Lemon Cake

This Almond Lemon Cake is light, fragrant, and naturally gluten-free, made with almond flour and fresh lemon juice for a refreshing dessert.

Ingredients:

- 2 cups (200g) almond flour
- 1/2 teaspoon baking powder
- 1/4 teaspoon salt
- 3 large eggs, separated
- 1/2 cup (100g) granulated sugar
- 1/4 cup (60ml) honey
- 1/4 cup (60ml) fresh lemon juice
- 1 tablespoon lemon zest
- 1 teaspoon vanilla extract

Instructions:

1. Preheat oven to 350°F (175°C). Grease an 8-inch round cake pan and line the bottom with parchment paper.

2. In a medium bowl, whisk almond flour, baking powder, and salt.

3. In a large bowl, beat egg yolks, sugar, honey, lemon juice, zest, and vanilla until smooth. Stir in the dry ingredients.

4. In a separate bowl, beat egg whites until stiff peaks form. Gently fold the egg whites into the batter in three additions.

5. Pour batter into the prepared pan and smooth the top. Bake for 25–30 minutes, or until a toothpick inserted in the center comes out clean.

6. Cool in the pan for 10 minutes before transferring to a wire rack.

Tips:

- Garnish with powdered sugar and sliced almonds for a simple presentation.

- Substitute orange juice and zest for a citrus variation.

Recipe 3: Gluten-Free Carrot Cake

Moist, spiced, and packed with carrots, this Gluten-Free Carrot Cake is a crowd-pleaser topped with luscious cream cheese frosting.

Ingredients for the Cake:

- 2 cups (250g) gluten-free all-purpose flour
- 1 teaspoon xanthan gum (if not included in the flour blend)
- 1 teaspoon baking powder
- 1 teaspoon baking soda
- 1 teaspoon cinnamon
- 1/4 teaspoon nutmeg
- 1/2 teaspoon salt
- 1 cup (200g) granulated sugar
- 1/2 cup (120ml) vegetable oil
- 1/2 cup (120ml) unsweetened applesauce
- 3 large eggs, room temperature
- 2 teaspoons vanilla extract
- 2 cups (200g) grated carrots
- 1/2 cup (60g) chopped walnuts or raisins (optional)

Ingredients for the Frosting:

- 8 oz (225g) cream cheese, softened
- 1/2 cup (115g) unsalted butter, softened

- 2 cups (250g) powdered sugar

- 1 teaspoon vanilla extract

Instructions:

1. Preheat oven to 350°F (175°C). Grease a 9x13-inch baking pan.

2. In a medium bowl, whisk flour, xanthan gum, baking powder, baking soda, cinnamon, nutmeg, and salt.

3. In a large bowl, beat sugar, oil, applesauce, eggs, and vanilla until smooth. Gradually add the dry ingredients, mixing until just combined. Fold in carrots and walnuts or raisins, if using.

4. Pour batter into the prepared pan and spread evenly. Bake for 30–35 minutes, or until a toothpick inserted in the center comes out clean. Cool completely.

5. For the frosting, beat cream cheese and butter until creamy. Gradually add powdered sugar and vanilla, mixing until smooth. Spread over the cooled cake.

Tips:

- Add crushed pineapple for extra moisture and sweetness.

- Top with toasted coconut or chopped nuts for added texture.

Flavor Combinations and Customizations

- Chocolate and Orange: Add orange zest to the Flourless Chocolate Cake for a citrus twist.

- Coconut and Lime: Replace lemon with lime in the Almond Lemon Cake and garnish with shredded coconut.

- Spiced Apple: Substitute grated apples for carrots in the Gluten-Free Carrot Cake and add a pinch of allspice.

Conclusion

Gluten-free cakes offer endless possibilities for creating desserts that are as delicious as their traditional counterparts. By understanding the nuances of alternative flours and incorporating techniques for moisture and structure, you can craft exceptional cakes that everyone will enjoy. Recipes like Flourless Chocolate Cake, Almond Lemon Cake, and Gluten-Free Carrot Cake showcase the diversity and potential of gluten-free baking, proving that dietary restrictions don't have to compromise flavor or texture. Let this chapter inspire you to explore new ingredients and techniques, opening up a world of gluten-free baking possibilities.

Chapter 7: Vegan Cakes

Vegan cakes are a testament to how delicious and indulgent desserts can be without relying on animal-based ingredients. They cater not only to those who follow a plant-based lifestyle but also to anyone seeking lighter, healthier, and more sustainable baking options. Crafting vegan cakes that everyone will love requires creativity, knowledge of ingredient substitutions, and a little bit of practice—but the results are worth it.

This chapter is your ultimate guide to vegan cake baking, featuring recipes for Vegan Chocolate Cake, Coconut Lime Cake, and Vegan Pumpkin Spice Cake. You'll also learn essential substitutions for eggs, butter, and dairy that maintain the flavor and texture of traditional cakes, ensuring that no one misses out on a slice of indulgence.

The Foundations of Vegan Cake Baking

1. What Makes a Cake Vegan?

A vegan cake contains no animal-derived ingredients such as eggs, butter, milk, or cream. Instead, plant-based alternatives are used to replicate the functionality of these traditional ingredients.

2. The Challenges of Vegan Baking

- Texture: Without eggs for structure, vegan cakes can sometimes become dense or crumbly.

- Moisture: Replacing butter and dairy can lead to dry cakes if not balanced properly.

- Flavor: Plant-based ingredients must complement each other to deliver a rich and satisfying taste.

Essential Substitutions for Vegan Cakes

1. Replacing Eggs

Eggs provide structure, moisture, and leavening in traditional cakes. These substitutes mimic their properties:

- Flaxseed or Chia Seed Egg: Mix 1 tablespoon ground flaxseed or chia seeds with 3 tablespoons water. Let sit for 5 minutes to form a gel.

- Applesauce: Use 1/4 cup unsweetened applesauce per egg. Adds moisture and a touch of sweetness.

- Mashed Bananas: Replace 1 egg with 1/4 cup mashed banana for moisture and natural sweetness.

- Silken Tofu: Use 1/4 cup blended silken tofu per egg for dense, creamy cakes.

- Baking Powder and Vinegar: Combine 1 tablespoon vinegar (apple cider or white) with 1 teaspoon baking powder for leavening.

2. Replacing Butter

Butter adds richness and flavor, but these substitutes work just as well:

- Vegan Butter or Margarine: Directly replace butter with plant-based alternatives.

- Coconut Oil: Use melted coconut oil for a rich texture. Choose refined coconut oil for a neutral flavor.

- Vegetable Oil: Adds moisture and softness without overpowering flavors.

3. Replacing Dairy

- Non-Dairy Milk: Almond, soy, oat, coconut, or cashew milk work as one-to-one substitutes for cow's milk.

- Non-Dairy Yogurt: Coconut or almond yogurt adds creaminess and tang.

- Coconut Cream: Whipped coconut cream makes an excellent substitute for heavy cream in frostings.

Tips for Successful Vegan Cake Baking

1. Balance the Wet and Dry Ingredients: Vegan cakes often require more liquid to achieve the right batter consistency.

2. Don't Overmix: Overmixing can lead to dense cakes. Mix just until combined.

3. Use Quality Ingredients: High-quality cocoa powder, vanilla extract, and spices elevate the flavor.

4. Layer Flavors: Incorporate extracts, zests, or spices to enhance depth and complexity.

5. Test for Doneness: Vegan cakes may take slightly longer to bake. Use a toothpick to ensure the center is cooked through.

Recipe 1: Vegan Chocolate Cake

Rich, moist, and utterly decadent, this Vegan Chocolate Cake is a foolproof recipe that will satisfy even the most ardent chocoholics.

Ingredients for the Cake:
- 1 3/4 cups (220g) all-purpose flour
- 3/4 cup (75g) unsweetened cocoa powder
- 1 1/2 teaspoons baking soda
- 1/2 teaspoon salt
- 1 1/2 cups (300g) granulated sugar
- 1 cup (240ml) non-dairy milk (e.g., almond or soy)
- 1/2 cup (120ml) vegetable oil
- 1 tablespoon apple cider vinegar
- 1 teaspoon vanilla extract
- 1 cup (240ml) hot coffee

Ingredients for the Frosting:
- 1/2 cup (115g) vegan butter, softened
- 2 1/2 cups (315g) powdered sugar
- 1/4 cup (25g) cocoa powder
- 3 tablespoons non-dairy milk
- 1 teaspoon vanilla extract

Instructions:

1. Preheat oven to 350°F (175°C). Grease and line two 9-inch round cake pans with parchment paper.

2. In a large bowl, sift together flour, cocoa powder, baking soda, and salt. Stir in sugar.

3. In a separate bowl, whisk non-dairy milk, oil, vinegar, and vanilla. Gradually add wet ingredients to the dry ingredients, mixing until smooth. Stir in hot coffee (the batter will be thin).

4. Divide batter evenly between the pans. Bake for 30–35 minutes, or until a toothpick inserted in the center comes out clean. Cool completely.

5. For the frosting, beat vegan butter until creamy. Gradually add powdered sugar and cocoa powder, alternating with non-dairy milk. Mix in vanilla. Frost the cooled cakes.

Tips:

- Add espresso powder to enhance the chocolate flavor.

- Garnish with fresh berries or shredded coconut.

Recipe 2: Coconut Lime Cake

This tropical-inspired Coconut Lime Cake is light, fluffy, and bursting with zesty citrus flavor and a hint of coconut.

Ingredients for the Cake:

- 2 cups (250g) all-purpose flour

- 1 teaspoon baking powder

- 1/2 teaspoon baking soda

- 1/2 teaspoon salt

- 1 cup (200g) granulated sugar

- 1/2 cup (120ml) coconut oil, melted

- 3/4 cup (180ml) coconut milk

- 1/4 cup (60ml) lime juice

- 1 tablespoon lime zest

- 1 teaspoon vanilla extract

Ingredients for the Frosting:

- 1/2 cup (115g) vegan butter, softened

- 2 cups (250g) powdered sugar

- 3 tablespoons coconut milk

- 1 teaspoon lime zest

Instructions:

1. Preheat oven to 350°F (175°C). Grease and line two 8-inch round cake pans.

2. In a medium bowl, whisk flour, baking powder, baking soda, and salt.

3. In a large bowl, whisk sugar and melted coconut oil. Add coconut milk, lime juice, lime zest, and vanilla, mixing until smooth. Gradually add dry ingredients, mixing until just combined.

4. Divide batter between the pans. Bake for 25–30 minutes, or until a toothpick comes out clean. Cool completely.

5. For the frosting, beat vegan butter until smooth. Gradually add powdered sugar, alternating with coconut milk. Mix in lime zest. Frost the cooled cakes.

Tips:

- Toast shredded coconut and sprinkle on top for added texture.

- Substitute lemon juice and zest for a citrus variation.

Recipe 3: Vegan Pumpkin Spice Cake

Perfect for autumn, this Vegan Pumpkin Spice Cake is spiced with cinnamon, nutmeg, and ginger, and topped with a creamy vegan frosting.

Ingredients for the Cake:

- 2 cups (250g) all-purpose flour
- 1 teaspoon baking powder
- 1 teaspoon baking soda
- 1 teaspoon cinnamon
- 1/2 teaspoon nutmeg
- 1/2 teaspoon ginger
- 1/4 teaspoon salt
- 1 cup (200g) granulated sugar
- 1/2 cup (120ml) vegetable oil
- 1 cup (240g) canned pumpkin puree
- 1/4 cup (60ml) applesauce
- 1 teaspoon vanilla extract

Ingredients for the Frosting:

- 1/2 cup (115g) vegan butter, softened
- 4 oz (115g) vegan cream cheese, softened
- 2 cups (250g) powdered sugar
- 1 teaspoon vanilla extract

Instructions:

1. Preheat oven to 350°F (175°C). Grease and line a 9x13-inch baking pan.

2. In a medium bowl, whisk flour, baking powder, baking soda, spices, and salt.

3. In a large bowl, whisk sugar, oil, pumpkin puree, applesauce, and vanilla. Gradually add dry ingredients, mixing until just combined.

4. Pour batter into the prepared pan and smooth the top. Bake for 30–35 minutes, or until a toothpick comes out clean. Cool completely.

5. For the frosting, beat vegan butter and cream cheese until smooth. Gradually add powdered sugar and vanilla, mixing until creamy. Spread over the cooled cake.

Tips:

- Add chopped walnuts or pecans for a crunchy texture.

- Sprinkle with cinnamon sugar for extra flavor.

Creative Flavor Combinations

- Chocolate and Raspberry: Add raspberry preserves between the layers of the Vegan Chocolate Cake.

- Coconut and Pineapple: Fold crushed pineapple into the Coconut Lime Cake batter for a tropical twist.

- Pumpkin and Maple: Drizzle Vegan Pumpkin Spice Cake with maple syrup for added sweetness.

Conclusion

Vegan cakes are a celebration of creativity and innovation, proving that plant-based desserts can be just as indulgent and flavorful as their traditional counterparts. By mastering key substitutions and experimenting with recipes like Vegan Chocolate Cake, Coconut Lime Cake, and Vegan Pumpkin Spice Cake, you'll have the tools to bake cakes that everyone will love, regardless of dietary preferences. Let this chapter inspire you to explore the endless possibilities of vegan baking, crafting cakes that are as kind to the planet as they are delicious.

Chapter 8: Specialty Cakes for Kids

Children's parties are an opportunity to create magical, memorable moments, and the cake often serves as the centerpiece of the celebration. Specialty cakes for kids go beyond flavor; they're about creativity, color, and fun. Whether it's a vibrant Rainbow Layer Cake, a fantastical Dinosaur Shaped Cake, or a playful Chocolate Funfetti Cake, the possibilities are endless.

This chapter guides you through the art of crafting cakes that delight children and adults alike. You'll find detailed recipes, tips for decorating, and inspiration for incorporating party themes into your designs.

Why Specialty Cakes Are Important for Kids' Parties

1. Creating Memorable Experiences

The cake often becomes the focal point of a child's birthday party. A beautifully designed cake that ties into their favorite theme—whether it's dinosaurs, rainbows, or superheroes—adds excitement and makes the event unforgettable.

2. Encouraging Creativity

Specialty cakes allow parents, bakers, and even kids to flex their creative muscles. From choosing colors and shapes to designing decorations, the process can be as fun as the final product.

3. Tailoring Cakes to Kids' Tastes

Kids love cakes that are visually appealing and packed with flavor. Specialty cakes combine vibrant decorations with delicious, crowd-pleasing flavors like chocolate, vanilla, and fruit.

Essential Tools for Kids' Cakes

1. Bakeware and Pans

   - Shaped Pans: Dinosaur, star, or heart-shaped pans eliminate the need for carving intricate designs.

- Round and Square Pans: Basic shapes can be stacked or carved to create custom designs.

2. Decorating Tools

- Piping Bags and Tips: Perfect for adding fine details like grass, stars, or lettering.

- Fondant Tools: Rollers, cutters, and embossers help create fondant shapes and textures.

- Spatulas and Smoothers: Essential for spreading and smoothing frosting.

3. Edible Decorations

- Sprinkles: Use for fun, colorful accents.

- Edible Glitter: Adds a magical sparkle.

- Fondant and Gum Paste: Ideal for creating figures and shapes.

- Food Coloring: Gel or liquid food coloring can transform batter, frosting, and fondant into vibrant hues.

Tips for Designing Kids' Cakes

1. Involve the Kids

Let children participate in choosing the theme, colors, and decorations. They'll be more excited to see (and eat) the final product.

2. Match the Party Theme

- For a space-themed party, add stars and planets to the cake.

- For an animal-themed celebration, craft fondant animals or use animal-shaped pans.

3. Focus on Color

Bright, bold colors appeal to kids. Use food coloring to create a rainbow effect or ombre frosting.

4. Keep it Simple

While intricate designs are beautiful, kids often appreciate playful simplicity. A dinosaur-shaped cake or a sprinkle-covered cupcake can be just as delightful as a multi-tiered masterpiece.

Recipe 1: Rainbow Layer Cake

A Rainbow Layer Cake is the ultimate showstopper, with vibrant, colorful layers that delight children when sliced.

Ingredients for the Cake:
- 3 cups (375g) all-purpose flour
- 1 tablespoon baking powder
- 1/2 teaspoon salt
- 1 cup (227g) unsalted butter, softened
- 2 cups (400g) granulated sugar
- 4 large eggs, room temperature
- 1 tablespoon vanilla extract
- 1 1/2 cups (360ml) whole milk, room temperature
- Gel food coloring (red, orange, yellow, green, blue, and purple)

Ingredients for the Frosting:
- 1 1/2 cups (340g) unsalted butter, softened
- 6 cups (750g) powdered sugar
- 1/4 cup (60ml) milk
- 1 tablespoon vanilla extract

Instructions:

1. Preheat the oven to 350°F (175°C). Grease and line six 8-inch round cake pans, or bake in batches if you have fewer pans.

2. In a medium bowl, whisk together flour, baking powder, and salt.

3. In a large bowl, cream butter and sugar until light and fluffy. Add eggs one at a time, then mix in vanilla.

4. Add dry ingredients in three additions, alternating with milk. Mix until smooth.

5. Divide batter evenly among six bowls. Add a few drops of gel food coloring to each bowl, creating red, orange, yellow, green, blue, and purple batters.

6. Pour each batter into a prepared pan. Bake for 18–22 minutes, or until a toothpick inserted in the center comes out clean. Cool completely.

7. For the frosting, beat butter until creamy. Gradually add powdered sugar, alternating with milk. Mix in vanilla.

8. Stack the cooled cake layers in rainbow order, spreading frosting between each layer. Cover the entire cake with a thin crumb coat and chill for 15 minutes. Apply a final layer of frosting.

Tips:
- Decorate with rainbow sprinkles, candy, or edible glitter for added flair.
- Use a serrated knife to level each layer for a more stable cake.

Recipe 2: Dinosaur Shaped Cake

This Dinosaur Shaped Cake transforms a simple round cake into a fun and ferocious dinosaur using clever carving and decoration.

Ingredients for the Cake:
- 2 1/2 cups (315g) all-purpose flour
- 2 teaspoons baking powder
- 1/2 teaspoon baking soda
- 1/4 teaspoon salt
- 1 cup (227g) unsalted butter, softened
- 1 3/4 cups (350g) granulated sugar
- 4 large eggs, room temperature
- 1 teaspoon vanilla extract
- 1 cup (240ml) buttermilk, room temperature

Ingredients for the Frosting:
- 1 cup (230g) unsalted butter, softened
- 4 cups (500g) powdered sugar
- 2–3 tablespoons milk
- 1 teaspoon vanilla extract
- Green gel food coloring

Instructions:

1. Preheat oven to 350°F (175°C). Grease and line two 9-inch round cake pans.

2. In a medium bowl, whisk flour, baking powder, baking soda, and salt.

3. In a large bowl, cream butter and sugar until fluffy. Add eggs one at a time, then mix in vanilla.

4. Add dry ingredients in three additions, alternating with buttermilk. Mix until smooth.

5. Divide batter evenly between the pans. Bake for 25–30 minutes, or until a toothpick comes out clean. Cool completely.

6. Carve one cake into a dinosaur body shape and the other into a tail, head, and legs.

7. For the frosting, beat butter until creamy. Gradually add powdered sugar, milk, and vanilla. Tint frosting green.

8. Assemble the dinosaur shape and frost the entire cake. Use piping bags to add texture (e.g., scales or spikes).

Tips:

- Add candy eyes or fondant decorations for extra character.

- Use chocolate cookies as "dirt" for the dinosaur to stand on.

Recipe 3: Chocolate Funfetti Cake

This Chocolate Funfetti Cake is a whimsical, sprinkle-filled delight with a rich chocolate base and colorful decorations.

Ingredients for the Cake:

- 2 cups (250g) all-purpose flour
- 3/4 cup (75g) unsweetened cocoa powder
- 2 teaspoons baking powder
- 1/2 teaspoon baking soda
- 1/4 teaspoon salt
- 1 cup (200g) granulated sugar
- 1/2 cup (120ml) vegetable oil
- 1 cup (240ml) buttermilk, room temperature
- 2 teaspoons vanilla extract
- 1/2 cup (100g) rainbow sprinkles

Ingredients for the Frosting:

- 1 cup (230g) unsalted butter, softened
- 4 cups (500g) powdered sugar
- 1/4 cup (60ml) milk
- 1 teaspoon vanilla extract

Instructions:

1. Preheat oven to 350°F (175°C). Grease and line two 9-inch round cake pans.

2. In a medium bowl, whisk flour, cocoa powder, baking powder, baking soda, and salt.

3. In a large bowl, whisk sugar, oil, buttermilk, and vanilla. Gradually add dry ingredients, mixing until smooth. Fold in sprinkles.

4. Divide batter evenly between the pans. Bake for 25–30 minutes, or until a toothpick comes out clean. Cool completely.

5. For the frosting, beat butter until creamy. Gradually add powdered sugar and milk. Mix in vanilla.

6. Frost the cakes and decorate with additional sprinkles.

Tips:

- Use chocolate ganache for a decadent topping.

- Add a sprinkle-filled surprise center by hollowing out the middle of one layer and filling it with sprinkles before assembling.

Creative Theme Ideas

1. Under the Sea: Use blue frosting, candy seashells, and fondant fish for a marine-themed cake.

2. Superheroes: Decorate with logos, colors, or shapes from popular superheroes.

3. Princess Party: Create a tiered cake with pastel colors, edible pearls, and tiara toppers.

Conclusion

Specialty cakes for kids bring joy, creativity, and fun to any celebration. Recipes like Rainbow Layer Cake, Dinosaur Shaped Cake, and Chocolate Funfetti Cake provide the foundation for crafting cakes that are as delicious as they are visually stunning. With the right tools, techniques, and imagination, you can create cakes that turn any child's party into an unforgettable experience. Let this chapter inspire you to embrace the magic of baking for kids, creating memories one slice at a time.

Chapter 9: Elegant Cakes for Adults

Elegant cakes are the epitome of sophistication, designed to please refined palates and elevate any special occasion. Unlike traditional birthday cakes or playful children's desserts, these cakes are crafted with layered flavors, artistic designs, and thoughtful pairings to create a memorable experience. Whether you're hosting a dinner party, celebrating an anniversary, or simply indulging in an exquisite dessert, elegant cakes add a touch of luxury to your table.

This chapter explores the art of baking sophisticated cakes for adults. We'll cover recipes for Earl Grey Lavender Cake, Black Forest Cake, and Champagne Raspberry Cake, as well as tips for pairing cakes with coffee, tea, and wine to create harmonious flavor combinations.

The Appeal of Elegant Cakes

1. Refined Flavors

Elegant cakes go beyond basic chocolate or vanilla, featuring unique ingredients like tea, liqueurs, floral essences, and fresh fruits to create complex and nuanced flavors.

2. Stunning Presentation

These cakes are as much about aesthetics as they are about taste. Think delicate frosting details, fresh flowers, gold leaf accents, and clean, modern designs.

3. Perfect for Special Occasions

Elegant cakes are ideal for weddings, anniversaries, dinner parties, or any gathering where a touch of class is required.

4. Pairing Opportunities

Their flavors often lend themselves beautifully to pairings with coffee, tea, or wine, enhancing the dining experience.

Tips for Baking Elegant Cakes

1. High-Quality Ingredients

- Use premium ingredients like European butter, high-quality chocolate, fresh cream, and organic extracts.

- Fresh, seasonal fruits and edible flowers elevate the flavor and presentation.

2. Balance of Flavors

- Balance sweetness with tanginess, bitterness, or spice.

- Incorporate complementary flavors, such as pairing citrus with floral notes or chocolate with fruit.

3. Master the Layers

- Elegant cakes often feature multiple layers. Ensure they're even for a polished look.

- Use fillings like curds, ganache, or mousse for added depth.

4. Focus on Decoration

- Use minimalist designs for modern elegance or intricate piping for a classic look.

- Garnish with fresh fruit, edible flowers, or decorative accents like macarons or gold leaf.

5. Pair Thoughtfully

- Match the cake's flavors with complementary beverages to enhance the overall experience.

Recipe 1: Earl Grey Lavender Cake

This Earl Grey Lavender Cake is a delicate and aromatic dessert, perfect for afternoon tea or a refined dinner party.

Ingredients for the Cake:

- 2 1/2 cups (315g) all-purpose flour
- 2 teaspoons baking powder
- 1/2 teaspoon baking soda
- 1/4 teaspoon salt
- 1 cup (227g) unsalted butter, softened
- 1 3/4 cups (350g) granulated sugar
- 4 large eggs, room temperature
- 1 cup (240ml) whole milk
- 4 Earl Grey tea bags or 2 tablespoons loose-leaf Earl Grey tea

- 1 tablespoon dried culinary lavender, finely ground
Ingredients for the Frosting:
- 1 cup (227g) unsalted butter, softened
- 4 cups (500g) powdered sugar
- 3 tablespoons heavy cream
- 1 teaspoon vanilla extract
- 1 teaspoon dried culinary lavender, finely ground
Instructions:
1. Preheat the oven to 350°F (175°C). Grease and line three 8-inch round cake pans.
2. Heat the milk until just simmering, then steep the Earl Grey tea for 5 minutes. Let cool to room temperature.
3. In a medium bowl, whisk together flour, baking powder, baking soda, and salt.
4. In a large bowl, cream butter and sugar until light and fluffy. Add eggs one at a time, mixing well after each addition.
5. Alternate adding the dry ingredients and the cooled tea-infused milk, beginning and ending with the dry ingredients. Stir in ground lavender.
6. Divide the batter evenly among the pans. Bake for 20–25 minutes, or until a toothpick inserted in the center comes out clean. Cool completely.
7. For the frosting, beat butter until creamy. Gradually add powdered sugar, heavy cream, vanilla, and ground lavender. Frost and layer the cooled cakes.
Tips:
- Decorate with fresh lavender sprigs or edible gold leaf for an elegant finish.
- Pair with Earl Grey tea or a dry white wine like Sauvignon Blanc.

Recipe 2: Black Forest Cake

A timeless classic, Black Forest Cake combines chocolate layers, whipped cream, and cherries for a decadent dessert with German origins.
Ingredients for the Cake:
- 1 3/4 cups (220g) all-purpose flour
- 3/4 cup (75g) unsweetened cocoa powder
- 1 1/2 teaspoons baking powder

- 1 teaspoon baking soda
- 1/2 teaspoon salt
- 1/2 cup (120ml) vegetable oil
- 1 3/4 cups (350g) granulated sugar
- 2 large eggs
- 1 teaspoon vanilla extract
- 1 cup (240ml) buttermilk
- 1/2 cup (120ml) hot coffee

Ingredients for the Filling and Topping:

- 2 cups (480ml) heavy cream
- 1/4 cup (30g) powdered sugar
- 1 teaspoon vanilla extract
- 1 cup (240ml) cherry preserves
- 1/2 cup (120ml) Kirsch (cherry brandy), optional
- Fresh cherries and chocolate shavings for garnish

Instructions:

1. Preheat oven to 350°F (175°C). Grease and line three 9-inch round cake pans.

2. In a medium bowl, sift together flour, cocoa powder, baking powder, baking soda, and salt.

3. In a large bowl, whisk oil, sugar, eggs, and vanilla until smooth. Alternate adding dry ingredients and buttermilk. Stir in hot coffee.

4. Divide batter among the pans. Bake for 25–30 minutes. Cool completely.

5. Whip heavy cream with powdered sugar and vanilla until stiff peaks form.

6. Brush each cake layer with Kirsch (if using). Spread cherry preserves and whipped cream between the layers. Frost the outside with whipped cream.

7. Decorate with fresh cherries and chocolate shavings.

Tips:

- Pair with a dark roast coffee or a rich red wine like Pinot Noir.
- Substitute Kirsch with cherry juice for an alcohol-free version.

Recipe 3: Champagne Raspberry Cake

This Champagne Raspberry Cake is light, airy, and perfect for celebrating special occasions like weddings or anniversaries.

Ingredients for the Cake:

- 2 1/2 cups (315g) cake flour
- 1 tablespoon baking powder
- 1/2 teaspoon salt
- 1 cup (227g) unsalted butter, softened
- 2 cups (400g) granulated sugar
- 4 large egg whites
- 1 teaspoon vanilla extract
- 1/2 cup (120ml) champagne or sparkling wine
- 1/2 cup (120ml) whole milk

Ingredients for the Frosting and Filling:

- 1 cup (227g) unsalted butter, softened
- 4 cups (500g) powdered sugar
- 1/4 cup (60ml) champagne
- 1/2 cup (150g) raspberry preserves
- Fresh raspberries for garnish

Instructions:

1. Preheat the oven to 350°F (175°C). Grease and line three 8-inch round cake pans.

2. In a medium bowl, whisk together flour, baking powder, and salt.

3. In a large bowl, cream butter and sugar until fluffy. Add egg whites and vanilla, mixing until smooth.

4. Alternate adding the dry ingredients with champagne and milk, beginning and ending with the dry ingredients.

5. Divide batter among the pans. Bake for 20–25 minutes, or until a toothpick comes out clean. Cool completely.

6. For the frosting, beat butter until creamy. Gradually add powdered sugar and champagne.

7. Spread raspberry preserves between the layers. Frost the cake and decorate with fresh raspberries.

Tips:

- Pair with a glass of champagne or sparkling rosé.
- Add edible gold leaf for an opulent touch.

Pairing Cakes with Beverages

1. Coffee

- Bold, dark coffees pair well with chocolate-based cakes like Black Forest Cake.

- Light roasts complement fruity or citrus-flavored cakes like Champagne Raspberry Cake.

2. Tea

- Earl Grey or lavender-infused cakes pair beautifully with black or green teas.

- Herbal teas with floral or citrus notes complement lighter cakes.

3. Wine

- Rich red wines like Merlot or Pinot Noir enhance the depth of chocolate cakes.

- Sparkling wines or Prosecco pair well with fruit-forward cakes.

Conclusion

Elegant cakes for adults combine exquisite flavors, stunning designs, and thoughtful pairings to create unforgettable desserts. Recipes like Earl Grey Lavender Cake, Black Forest Cake, and Champagne Raspberry Cake highlight the artistry and creativity involved in crafting cakes for refined tastes. With premium ingredients, attention to detail, and a touch of creativity, you can transform any occasion into a sophisticated celebration. Let this chapter inspire you to explore the world of elegant cakes, where every slice is a masterpiece.

Chapter 10: Holiday and Seasonal Cakes

The changing seasons and festive holidays present endless opportunities to celebrate with cakes. Holiday and seasonal cakes go beyond flavor—they evoke emotions, memories, and traditions tied to the time of year. Whether it's a spiced and snowy Christmas Yule Log, a spooky Halloween Pumpkin Cake, or a cheerful Easter Lemon Bunny Cake, these desserts are as much about creating joy as they are about satisfying taste buds.

This chapter explores the art of crafting cakes that capture the essence of each season and holiday. It includes recipes for three iconic cakes, along with decorating ideas to bring the spirit of the occasion to life.

The Joy of Holiday and Seasonal Cakes

1. Symbolizing the Season

Holiday cakes often feature flavors and decorations that reflect the essence of the season, such as warm spices for winter, citrus for spring, and pumpkin for autumn.

2. Creating Traditions

Many families bake the same holiday cakes year after year, turning them into cherished traditions passed down through generations.

3. Adding a Personal Touch

Seasonal cakes provide a canvas for creativity. Whether you're using edible decorations, festive colors, or intricate designs, these cakes can be tailored to suit any celebration.

4. Perfect Centerpieces

A well-decorated holiday cake doubles as a showstopping centerpiece, adding a touch of magic to any table.

Essential Tools for Holiday and Seasonal Cakes

1. Seasonal Bakeware

   - Shaped pans (e.g., bunny, pumpkin, or snowflake) make it easy to create themed cakes.
   - Silicone molds for smaller edible decorations.

2. Decorating Supplies
- Piping bags and tips for intricate designs.
- Edible glitter, sprinkles, and gold leaf for festive flair.
- Food-safe stencils for creating seasonal patterns with powdered sugar or cocoa powder.
3. Food Coloring
- Gel food coloring for vibrant hues to match holiday themes.

Recipe 1: Christmas Yule Log (Bûche de Noël)

The Yule Log, or Bûche de Noël, is a classic French dessert that represents a traditional log burned during the winter solstice. This rolled cake combines rich chocolate sponge with a creamy filling and a stunning wood-like decoration.

Ingredients for the Cake:
- 3/4 cup (95g) all-purpose flour
- 1/4 cup (25g) unsweetened cocoa powder
- 1 teaspoon baking powder
- 1/4 teaspoon salt
- 4 large eggs, separated
- 3/4 cup (150g) granulated sugar
- 1 teaspoon vanilla extract
- 1/4 cup (60ml) milk

Ingredients for the Filling:
- 1 cup (240ml) heavy cream
- 2 tablespoons powdered sugar
- 1 teaspoon vanilla extract

Ingredients for the Frosting:
- 1/2 cup (115g) unsalted butter, softened
- 2 cups (250g) powdered sugar
- 1/4 cup (25g) cocoa powder
- 2–3 tablespoons milk
- 1 teaspoon vanilla extract

Instructions:

1. Preheat oven to 350°F (175°C). Line a 15x10-inch jelly roll pan with parchment paper.

2. In a medium bowl, sift together flour, cocoa powder, baking powder, and salt.

3. In a large bowl, beat egg yolks and 1/2 cup sugar until thick and pale. Stir in vanilla and milk.

4. In a separate bowl, beat egg whites until foamy. Gradually add the remaining 1/4 cup sugar and beat until stiff peaks form.

5. Gently fold the dry ingredients into the yolk mixture, then fold in the egg whites.

6. Spread the batter evenly in the prepared pan. Bake for 12–15 minutes, or until the cake springs back when touched.

7. While warm, roll the cake (with the parchment paper) into a log. Cool completely.

8. For the filling, whip heavy cream with powdered sugar and vanilla until stiff peaks form. Unroll the cake, spread the filling, and re-roll.

9. For the frosting, beat butter, powdered sugar, cocoa powder, milk, and vanilla until smooth. Frost the outside of the log, then use a fork to create a woodgrain texture.

10. Decorate with meringue mushrooms, powdered sugar "snow," or fresh cranberries and rosemary sprigs.

Tips:

- Chill the frosted cake before serving for cleaner slices.

- Pair with a spiced latte or mulled wine.

Recipe 2: Halloween Pumpkin Cake

This Halloween Pumpkin Cake is moist, spiced, and shaped like a pumpkin, making it the perfect dessert for spooky celebrations.

Ingredients for the Cake:

- 2 1/2 cups (315g) all-purpose flour
- 2 teaspoons baking powder
- 1 teaspoon baking soda
- 1 teaspoon cinnamon
- 1/2 teaspoon nutmeg

- 1/4 teaspoon cloves
- 1/2 teaspoon salt
- 1 cup (200g) granulated sugar
- 1/2 cup (100g) brown sugar
- 1/2 cup (120ml) vegetable oil
- 1/2 cup (120ml) unsweetened applesauce
- 1 cup (240g) canned pumpkin puree
- 3 large eggs
- 1 teaspoon vanilla extract

Ingredients for the Frosting:
- 1 cup (227g) unsalted butter, softened
- 4 cups (500g) powdered sugar
- 2–3 tablespoons milk
- 1 teaspoon vanilla extract
- Orange and green gel food coloring

Instructions:

1. Preheat oven to 350°F (175°C). Grease and flour two Bundt pans.

2. In a medium bowl, whisk together flour, baking powder, baking soda, spices, and salt.

3. In a large bowl, beat sugars, oil, applesauce, pumpkin puree, eggs, and vanilla until smooth. Gradually add the dry ingredients.

4. Divide batter evenly between the Bundt pans. Bake for 30–35 minutes, or until a toothpick comes out clean. Cool completely.

5. For the frosting, beat butter, powdered sugar, milk, and vanilla until smooth. Tint most of the frosting orange and a small portion green.

6. To assemble, stack the Bundt cakes flat sides together to form a pumpkin shape. Frost with orange frosting and use green frosting for the stem.

Tips:
- Add candy eyes or a carved jack-o'-lantern face for extra spookiness.
- Serve with hot apple cider.

Recipe 3: Easter Lemon Bunny Cake

This light and zesty Easter Lemon Bunny Cake is shaped like a bunny, making it a charming addition to your spring celebrations.

Ingredients for the Cake:
- 2 1/2 cups (315g) all-purpose flour
- 2 teaspoons baking powder
- 1/2 teaspoon baking soda
- 1/4 teaspoon salt
- 1 cup (227g) unsalted butter, softened
- 2 cups (400g) granulated sugar
- 4 large eggs
- 1 tablespoon lemon zest
- 1/2 cup (120ml) lemon juice
- 1 cup (240ml) buttermilk

Ingredients for the Frosting:
- 1 cup (227g) unsalted butter, softened
- 4 cups (500g) powdered sugar
- 1/4 cup (60ml) lemon juice
- 1 teaspoon vanilla extract

Instructions:

1. Preheat oven to 350°F (175°C). Grease and flour two round 9-inch cake pans.

2. In a medium bowl, whisk flour, baking powder, baking soda, and salt.

3. In a large bowl, cream butter and sugar until light and fluffy. Add eggs one at a time, then mix in lemon zest and juice.

4. Alternate adding dry ingredients and buttermilk, beginning and ending with the dry ingredients.

5. Divide batter evenly between the pans. Bake for 25–30 minutes. Cool completely.

6. For the frosting, beat butter, powdered sugar, lemon juice, and vanilla until smooth.

7. To assemble, cut one round cake into ear shapes and place them around the other round cake to form a bunny shape. Frost and decorate with candy eyes, a licorice nose, and coconut "fur."

Tips:
- Use pastel-colored frosting for a more festive look.
- Serve with a pot of chamomile tea.

Decorating Ideas for Seasonal Flair

1. Winter (Christmas)
   - Dust cakes with powdered sugar for a snowy effect.
   - Use edible glitter or gold leaf for a luxurious touch.
   2. Autumn (Halloween)
   - Add candy pumpkins, bats, or ghosts.
   - Use black and orange frosting for spooky details.
   3. Spring (Easter)
   - Decorate with pastel shades, fresh flowers, or candy eggs.
   - Create grass effects with green-tinted coconut flakes.

Conclusion

Holiday and seasonal cakes bring joy, flavor, and festivity to every celebration. Recipes like the Christmas Yule Log, Halloween Pumpkin Cake, and Easter Lemon Bunny Cake capture the essence of their respective holidays while providing opportunities for creative expression. By mastering these cakes and experimenting with decorations, you can make each season a little sweeter and every celebration unforgettable. Let this chapter inspire you to embrace the magic of seasonal baking, one cake at a time.

Chapter 11: Ice Cream and Frozen Cakes

Ice cream and frozen cakes are the perfect fusion of two beloved desserts. Combining the creamy, cool textures of ice cream or sorbet with the decadent flavors of cake creates indulgent treats that are ideal for celebrations or a sweet escape from the heat. Whether it's the nostalgic appeal of a Classic Ice Cream Cake, the elegant layers of a Frozen Tiramisu Cake, or the refreshing burst of a Mango Sorbet Cake, frozen cakes are versatile, creative, and crowd-pleasing.

This chapter explores the art of crafting frozen cakes, with recipes and tips for assembling, decorating, and storing them. By mastering the techniques and recipes, you can create frozen cakes that look as good as they taste.

Why Frozen Cakes?

1. A Cool Twist on Tradition

Frozen cakes offer a refreshing alternative to traditional baked cakes, making them especially appealing in warmer months.

2. Endless Flavor Possibilities

The combination of cake and frozen elements like ice cream or sorbet opens up endless flavor options, from classic pairings to adventurous combinations.

3. Easy Make-Ahead Desserts

Frozen cakes can be prepared ahead of time and stored until needed, making them ideal for parties and gatherings.

4. Stunning Presentation

Frozen cakes are visually striking, with layers of cake, frozen fillings, and decorative toppings that elevate any dessert table.

Essential Tools for Frozen Cakes

1. Springform Pans

   - Essential for easy removal and maintaining neat layers. Choose sizes that suit your desired cake dimensions.

2. Offset Spatula

   - For spreading layers evenly and smoothing the surface.

3. Parchment Paper or Plastic Wrap

- Lines pans for easy removal and protects frozen cakes during storage.

4. Cake Ring or Acetate Strips

- Helps achieve clean, sharp edges when assembling multi-layer frozen cakes.

5. Freezer-Safe Containers

- Protects cakes from freezer burn during storage.

Tips for Assembling and Storing Frozen Cakes

1. Layering Techniques

- Allow each layer to freeze solid before adding the next to maintain clean, defined layers.

- Use thin layers of cake to avoid overpowering the frozen elements.

2. Timing and Patience

- Plan ahead, as frozen cakes require several hours (or overnight) to set properly.

3. Storage

- Wrap cakes tightly in plastic wrap or store in an airtight container to prevent freezer burn.

- Add decorative elements like whipped cream or fresh fruit just before serving.

4. Serving

- Let frozen cakes sit at room temperature for 10–15 minutes before slicing for easier serving.

Recipe 1: Classic Ice Cream Cake

A timeless dessert, the Classic Ice Cream Cake layers rich chocolate and vanilla ice cream with chocolate cookie crumbles and whipped cream frosting.

Ingredients:

- 1 1/2 quarts (1.4L) chocolate ice cream, softened
- 1 1/2 quarts (1.4L) vanilla ice cream, softened
- 2 cups (200g) chocolate cookie crumbs
- 1/4 cup (60g) melted butter

- 2 cups (480ml) heavy whipping cream
- 1/2 cup (60g) powdered sugar
- 1 teaspoon vanilla extract
- Chocolate syrup or sprinkles for decoration

Instructions:

1. Line a 9-inch springform pan with plastic wrap, leaving overhang for easy removal.

2. Mix cookie crumbs with melted butter and press into the bottom of the pan to form a crust. Freeze for 15 minutes.

3. Spread softened chocolate ice cream over the crust. Smooth with an offset spatula and freeze for 30 minutes.

4. Add a layer of vanilla ice cream, smoothing the top. Freeze for at least 2 hours or overnight.

5. Whip heavy cream, powdered sugar, and vanilla until stiff peaks form. Spread over the frozen cake.

6. Decorate with chocolate syrup or sprinkles. Return to the freezer for 1 hour before serving.

Tips:

- Substitute the cookie crust with brownie or cake layers for variation.
- Add crushed candy bars or nuts between layers for extra texture.

Recipe 2: Frozen Tiramisu Cake

This Frozen Tiramisu Cake combines the flavors of coffee, mascarpone, and chocolate for an elegant and indulgent dessert.

Ingredients:

- 1 cup (240ml) brewed espresso, cooled
- 1/4 cup (60ml) coffee liqueur (optional)
- 24 ladyfingers
- 2 cups (480ml) heavy cream, whipped to stiff peaks
- 1 cup (225g) mascarpone cheese
- 1/2 cup (100g) granulated sugar
- 1 teaspoon vanilla extract

- 1/2 cup (60g) cocoa powder
- Chocolate shavings for garnish

Instructions:

1. Combine espresso and coffee liqueur in a shallow dish. Dip each ladyfinger briefly in the mixture and arrange them to cover the bottom of a 9-inch springform pan.

2. In a bowl, mix mascarpone, sugar, and vanilla until smooth. Gently fold in whipped cream.

3. Spread half the mascarpone mixture over the ladyfingers. Sift cocoa powder on top.

4. Add another layer of dipped ladyfingers, then top with the remaining mascarpone mixture. Smooth the top and freeze for at least 4 hours or overnight.

5. Before serving, dust with cocoa powder and garnish with chocolate shavings.

Tips:

- Replace ladyfingers with sponge cake for a softer texture.
- Serve with espresso or cappuccino for a classic pairing.

Recipe 3: Mango Sorbet Cake

Bright, refreshing, and perfect for summer, this Mango Sorbet Cake layers tropical sorbet with a light vanilla cake base.

Ingredients:

- 1 quart (950ml) mango sorbet, softened
- 1 1/2 cups (180g) all-purpose flour
- 1 teaspoon baking powder
- 1/2 teaspoon baking soda
- 1/4 teaspoon salt
- 1/2 cup (115g) unsalted butter, softened
- 3/4 cup (150g) granulated sugar
- 2 large eggs, room temperature
- 1 teaspoon vanilla extract
- 1/2 cup (120ml) buttermilk, room temperature

- Fresh mango slices for garnish

Instructions:

1. Preheat oven to 350°F (175°C). Grease and line an 8-inch round cake pan.

2. In a medium bowl, whisk together flour, baking powder, baking soda, and salt.

3. In a large bowl, cream butter and sugar until fluffy. Add eggs one at a time, then mix in vanilla.

4. Alternate adding dry ingredients and buttermilk, mixing until smooth. Pour batter into the pan and bake for 20–25 minutes. Cool completely.

5. Line a springform pan with plastic wrap. Place the cake layer at the bottom and spread softened mango sorbet on top. Smooth the surface and freeze for at least 4 hours or overnight.

6. Garnish with fresh mango slices before serving.

Tips:

- Substitute mango sorbet with raspberry or passion fruit sorbet for a different flavor profile.

- Pair with a sparkling wine or tropical cocktail.

Creative Decorating Ideas

1. Seasonal Touches

- Use fresh fruits, edible flowers, or colored sprinkles to match the season or occasion.

2. Textural Elements

- Add crunch with cookie crumbs, chocolate shavings, or crushed nuts.

3. Elegant Finishes

- Drizzle with sauces like chocolate ganache or fruit coulis for a polished look.

4. Layered Colors

- Use contrasting ice cream or sorbet flavors for vibrant layers when sliced.

Conclusion

Ice cream and frozen cakes bring together the best of both worlds, offering creamy textures and bold flavors in visually stunning desserts. Recipes like Classic Ice Cream Cake, Frozen Tiramisu Cake, and Mango Sorbet Cake showcase the versatility of these confections, making them perfect for any occasion. By following the tips and techniques outlined in this chapter, you can craft frozen cakes that not only taste incredible but also become the highlight of your celebrations. Let this chapter inspire you to explore the cool and creative world of frozen desserts, where every slice is a masterpiece.

Chapter 12: Healthy and Wholesome Cakes

Cakes have always been a symbol of indulgence, but they don't have to be loaded with sugar and processed ingredients to be delicious. Healthy and wholesome cakes are a growing trend in baking, focusing on balancing flavor with nutrition. By using whole grains, natural sweeteners, and nutrient-rich ingredients, you can create cakes that satisfy your sweet tooth while providing nourishment.

This chapter delves into the art of creating healthy cakes, offering recipes for Whole Wheat Banana Cake, Low-Sugar Apple Cake, and Oatmeal Breakfast Cake. You'll also learn how to incorporate wholesome ingredients, reduce sugar, and make cakes that are as good for your body as they are for your taste buds.

The Philosophy of Healthy Baking

1. Why Healthy Cakes?

- Nourishing Ingredients: Healthy cakes include whole foods like fruits, nuts, and whole grains, offering vitamins, minerals, and fiber.

- Reduced Sugar: Cutting back on refined sugar helps manage energy levels and avoids sugar crashes.

- Dietary Inclusivity: Many wholesome cakes cater to special diets, such as gluten-free, dairy-free, or low-sugar lifestyles.

2. The Challenge of Healthy Cakes

- Flavor Balance: Reducing sugar and fat can affect taste and texture, requiring thoughtful substitutions.

- Texture Adjustments: Whole grain flours and natural sweeteners behave differently than their processed counterparts.

Wholesome Ingredients for Healthy Cakes

1. Whole Grain Flours

- Whole Wheat Flour: Adds fiber, nutrients, and a nutty flavor. Best paired with moist ingredients to balance density.

- Oat Flour: Gluten-free and naturally sweet, it works well in breakfast cakes and dense bakes.

- Almond Flour: High in protein and healthy fats, it adds moisture and a soft texture.

2. Natural Sweeteners

- Honey: Adds moisture and a subtle floral flavor.

- Maple Syrup: A robust, natural sweetener with a distinctive taste.

- Coconut Sugar: A lower-glycemic alternative to granulated sugar, with a caramel-like flavor.

- Mashed Fruits: Bananas, apples, and dates can sweeten cakes naturally while adding moisture.

3. Healthy Fats

- Avocado: Replaces butter for a creamy texture.

- Coconut Oil: A plant-based fat that works well in most recipes.

- Greek Yogurt: Adds protein, moisture, and a tangy flavor.

4. Add-ins for Nutrition

- Nuts and Seeds: Walnuts, almonds, chia seeds, and flaxseeds add crunch and healthy fats.

- Vegetables: Zucchini, carrots, and sweet potatoes boost moisture and nutrients.

- Spices: Cinnamon, nutmeg, and ginger enhance flavor without added sugar.

Tips for Healthy Baking

1. Balance Wet and Dry Ingredients: Whole grain flours absorb more liquid, so increase wet ingredients as needed.

2. Don't Overmix: Overmixing can make cakes dense. Stir until just combined.

3. Use Natural Flavors: Incorporate zests, spices, or extracts to enhance taste without added sugar.

4. Watch Baking Times: Healthier cakes can dry out faster. Check for doneness early.

5. Taste as You Go: Adjust sweetness and spice levels to suit your preference.

Recipe 1: Whole Wheat Banana Cake

This Whole Wheat Banana Cake is naturally sweetened with ripe bananas and honey, making it a guilt-free treat for any time of day.

Ingredients for the Cake:

- 2 cups (250g) whole wheat flour
- 1 teaspoon baking soda
- 1/2 teaspoon baking powder
- 1/4 teaspoon salt
- 1 teaspoon cinnamon
- 1/2 cup (120ml) coconut oil, melted
- 1/3 cup (80ml) honey or maple syrup
- 2 large eggs, room temperature
- 1 teaspoon vanilla extract
- 3 ripe bananas, mashed
- 1/2 cup (120ml) plain Greek yogurt

Optional Toppings:

- Chopped walnuts or pecans
- Unsweetened shredded coconut

Instructions:

1. Preheat oven to 350°F (175°C). Grease and flour an 8-inch square pan.

2. In a medium bowl, whisk together flour, baking soda, baking powder, salt, and cinnamon.

3. In a large bowl, whisk coconut oil, honey, eggs, and vanilla until smooth. Stir in mashed bananas and yogurt.

4. Gradually add dry ingredients to wet ingredients, mixing until just combined.

5. Pour batter into the prepared pan. Sprinkle with nuts or coconut if desired.

6. Bake for 30–35 minutes, or until a toothpick inserted in the center comes out clean. Cool before slicing.

Tips:

- Replace some of the banana with grated zucchini for added moisture.
- Serve with a dollop of Greek yogurt or nut butter for extra protein.

Recipe 2: Low-Sugar Apple Cake

This Low-Sugar Apple Cake uses fresh apples and a touch of cinnamon for natural sweetness, making it a perfect fall dessert.

Ingredients:

- 1 1/2 cups (190g) all-purpose flour or spelt flour
- 1 teaspoon baking powder
- 1/2 teaspoon baking soda
- 1/4 teaspoon salt
- 1 teaspoon cinnamon
- 1/2 teaspoon nutmeg
- 1/4 cup (60ml) olive oil
- 1/4 cup (60ml) applesauce
- 1/4 cup (50g) coconut sugar
- 2 large eggs, room temperature
- 1 teaspoon vanilla extract
- 2 cups (240g) peeled and chopped apples
- 1/4 cup (30g) chopped walnuts or raisins (optional)

Instructions:

1. Preheat oven to 350°F (175°C). Grease and line a 9-inch round cake pan.

2. In a medium bowl, whisk flour, baking powder, baking soda, salt, cinnamon, and nutmeg.

3. In a large bowl, whisk olive oil, applesauce, coconut sugar, eggs, and vanilla until well combined.

4. Gradually add dry ingredients to wet ingredients, mixing until just combined. Fold in apples and walnuts or raisins, if using.

5. Pour batter into the prepared pan. Bake for 30–35 minutes, or until a toothpick comes out clean. Cool before serving.

Tips:

- Serve warm with a drizzle of maple syrup or a dollop of whipped coconut cream.

- Use pears instead of apples for a seasonal variation.

Recipe 3: Oatmeal Breakfast Cake

This Oatmeal Breakfast Cake is packed with fiber and nutrients, making it a wholesome start to your day.

Ingredients:

- 2 cups (200g) rolled oats
- 1 cup (240ml) unsweetened almond milk
- 1/4 cup (60ml) maple syrup
- 1/4 cup (60ml) coconut oil, melted
- 2 large eggs or flax eggs
- 1 teaspoon vanilla extract
- 1 teaspoon baking powder
- 1/2 teaspoon baking soda
- 1/4 teaspoon salt
- 1/2 teaspoon cinnamon
- 1/2 cup (120g) mashed banana or unsweetened applesauce
- 1/4 cup (30g) dark chocolate chips or dried fruit

Instructions:

1. Preheat oven to 350°F (175°C). Grease and line an 8-inch square pan.

2. In a large bowl, mix oats, almond milk, maple syrup, coconut oil, eggs, and vanilla. Let sit for 10 minutes.

3. Stir in baking powder, baking soda, salt, cinnamon, and mashed banana or applesauce. Fold in chocolate chips or dried fruit.

4. Pour batter into the prepared pan and smooth the top. Bake for 25–30 minutes, or until golden and set. Cool before slicing.

Tips:

- Replace chocolate chips with nuts or seeds for a nutty variation.
- Store slices in the fridge for a quick grab-and-go breakfast.

Creative Substitutions and Variations

- Sweeteners: Swap honey with agave or date syrup for a different flavor.
- Flours: Mix whole wheat and almond flour for lighter cakes.

- Fruits and Veggies: Experiment with grated carrots, zucchini, or sweet potatoes for added nutrients.

Conclusion

Healthy and wholesome cakes prove that desserts can be both nutritious and delicious. Recipes like Whole Wheat Banana Cake, Low-Sugar Apple Cake, and Oatmeal Breakfast Cake showcase how natural ingredients and creative techniques can transform traditional baking into something guilt-free and satisfying. By using whole grains, natural sweeteners, and nutrient-rich add-ins, you can create cakes that nourish both the body and the soul. Let this chapter inspire you to bake cakes that prioritize health without compromising flavor, making every slice a wholesome indulgence.

Chapter 13: Cakes from Around the World

Cakes are a universal expression of celebration, comfort, and tradition, yet their flavors, textures, and preparation methods vary widely across cultures. Exploring global cake traditions allows us to appreciate the artistry and history behind each unique creation. From the delicate layers of a French Opera Cake to the festive charm of Italian Panettone, and the earthy elegance of a Japanese Matcha Roll Cake, cakes from around the world highlight the diversity of baking.

This chapter delves into the origins and techniques of these international cakes, offering recipes adapted for home bakers. By understanding the cultural significance and traditional preparation of these cakes, you'll gain new skills and flavors to enrich your baking repertoire.

The Importance of Global Cake Traditions

1. Cultural Significance
    - Cakes often symbolize milestones, holidays, and traditions, reflecting the history and values of a region.
    2. Diverse Ingredients and Techniques
    - Each culture brings its unique ingredients and baking techniques, from the use of green tea in Japanese desserts to the incorporation of coffee in French pastries.
    3. Connecting Through Food
    - Baking cakes from different countries allows us to experience other cultures and share them with others, fostering a sense of global connection.

Tips for Adapting Global Cake Recipes for Home Baking

1. Sourcing Ingredients
    - Specialty ingredients like matcha powder, Italian candied fruits, or almond paste can often be found in international grocery stores or online.

- If unavailable, substitute with locally accessible ingredients that mimic the original flavor profile.

2. Simplifying Techniques

- Complex recipes can be simplified without losing their essence by streamlining steps or using modern tools like stand mixers.

3. Adjusting for Preferences

- Adapt recipes to suit dietary preferences or ingredient availability without compromising authenticity.

4. Practicing Patience

- Many traditional cakes, like Opera Cake or Panettone, require time and precision. Approach them as a rewarding baking journey rather than a rushed task.

Recipe 1: Japanese Matcha Roll Cake

The Japanese Matcha Roll Cake is a light, fluffy dessert with a vibrant green tea flavor and a creamy filling, embodying the delicate artistry of Japanese baking.

Ingredients for the Cake:

- 4 large eggs, separated
- 1/2 cup (100g) granulated sugar
- 1 tablespoon honey
- 1/2 cup (65g) cake flour
- 1 tablespoon matcha powder
- 1/4 teaspoon salt

Ingredients for the Filling:

- 1 cup (240ml) heavy cream
- 2 tablespoons powdered sugar
- 1 teaspoon vanilla extract

Instructions:

1. Preheat the oven to 350°F (175°C). Line a 10x15-inch jelly roll pan with parchment paper.

2. In a bowl, beat egg yolks, 1/4 cup sugar, and honey until pale and thick.

3. Sift cake flour, matcha powder, and salt into the yolk mixture. Fold gently to combine.

4. In a separate bowl, beat egg whites until frothy. Gradually add the remaining 1/4 cup sugar, beating until stiff peaks form.

5. Fold the egg whites into the yolk mixture in three additions, taking care not to deflate the batter.

6. Pour the batter into the prepared pan and spread evenly. Bake for 12–15 minutes, or until the cake springs back when touched.

7. Let the cake cool slightly, then roll it (with the parchment paper) into a log. Cool completely.

8. For the filling, whip heavy cream, powdered sugar, and vanilla until stiff peaks form. Unroll the cake, spread the cream, and re-roll. Refrigerate for 1 hour before slicing.

Tips:

- Dust the roll with powdered sugar or extra matcha powder for garnish.

- Pair with a cup of matcha tea for a complete experience.

Recipe 2: French Opera Cake

The French Opera Cake is a luxurious layered dessert featuring almond sponge, coffee buttercream, and chocolate ganache, perfect for special occasions.

*KIngredients for the Joconde Sponge:

- 6 large eggs

- 6 large egg whites

- 1 cup (100g) almond flour

- 1 cup (125g) powdered sugar

- 1/4 cup (30g) all-purpose flour

- 1/4 cup (50g) granulated sugar

Ingredients for the Coffee Buttercream:

- 3 large egg yolks

- 1/2 cup (100g) granulated sugar

- 1/4 cup (60ml) water

- 1 cup (227g) unsalted butter, softened

- 1 tablespoon espresso powder dissolved in 1 tablespoon hot water

Ingredients for the Ganache:

- 1/2 cup (120ml) heavy cream

- 8 oz (225g) dark chocolate, chopped

Ingredients for Assembly:
- 1/2 cup (120ml) strong brewed coffee, cooled
Instructions:
1. Joconde Sponge: Preheat oven to 400°F (200°C). Line three 10x15-inch pans with parchment paper. Beat eggs, almond flour, and powdered sugar until thick. Fold in flour. In a separate bowl, beat egg whites and granulated sugar until stiff. Fold into the almond mixture. Spread batter evenly into the pans and bake for 5–7 minutes. Cool completely.

2. Buttercream: Whisk yolks in a bowl. In a saucepan, heat sugar and water until it reaches 240°F (115°C). Gradually pour the syrup into the yolks while whisking. Beat until cooled. Add butter, a piece at a time, and espresso, beating until smooth.

3. Ganache: Heat cream until just simmering. Pour over chopped chocolate and stir until smooth.

4. Assembly: Place one layer of sponge on a serving tray. Brush with coffee. Spread a layer of buttercream. Repeat with remaining layers. Spread ganache on top. Chill for 1 hour before slicing.

Tips:
- Use acetate strips for clean edges.
- Serve with espresso or dessert wine.

Recipe 3: Italian Panettone

Panettone is a tall, sweet bread filled with dried fruits and candied citrus, traditionally enjoyed during Christmas in Italy.

Ingredients:
- 3 cups (375g) all-purpose flour
- 1/4 cup (50g) granulated sugar
- 1/4 teaspoon salt
- 1 tablespoon instant yeast
- 2 large eggs, room temperature
- 1/4 cup (60ml) warm milk
- 1/4 cup (60g) unsalted butter, softened
- 1/2 cup (75g) dried fruit (raisins, cranberries)
- 1/4 cup (50g) candied orange peel

- 1 teaspoon vanilla extract

Instructions:

1. In a large bowl, mix flour, sugar, salt, and yeast. Add eggs, milk, butter, and vanilla. Knead until smooth. Cover and let rise until doubled, about 1 hour.

2. Knead in dried fruits and orange peel. Shape into a ball and place in a greased Panettone mold or tall, round baking dish. Let rise until doubled.

3. Preheat oven to 350°F (175°C). Bake for 35–40 minutes, or until golden. Cool before slicing.

Tips:

- Substitute dried fruits with chocolate chips for a modern twist.

- Serve with sweet wine or coffee.

Exploring More Global Cakes

- German Baumkuchen: A layered "tree cake" baked on a rotating spit.

- Mexican Tres Leches Cake: A sponge cake soaked in three types of milk.

- Indian Mawa Cake: A dense, cardamom-spiced cake made with evaporated milk solids.

Conclusion

Cakes from around the world celebrate cultural diversity and the art of baking. Recipes like Japanese Matcha Roll Cake, French Opera Cake, and Italian Panettone showcase the rich history and flavors of international desserts. By adapting these recipes for home kitchens, you can embark on a global baking adventure, bringing the tastes and traditions of different countries to your table. Let this chapter inspire you to explore, experiment, and savor the world one slice at a time.

Chapter 14: Advanced Decorating Techniques

Decorating a cake is both an art and a science. While baking sets the foundation, it's the decoration that transforms a simple cake into a masterpiece. Advanced decorating techniques—like piping intricate designs, working with fondant, and crafting delicate sugar flowers—allow bakers to create professional-quality cakes suitable for weddings, birthdays, and other special occasions. Whether you're building a tiered cake or adding the finishing touches to a single-layer masterpiece, these techniques will elevate your cakes to the next level.

This chapter covers essential tips, tricks, and advanced techniques for decorating cakes, with a focus on professional-quality designs. From mastering piping and fondant work to building tiered cakes, you'll learn how to craft stunning creations that are as beautiful as they are delicious.

The Importance of Cake Decoration

1. Visual Appeal
    - A beautifully decorated cake creates a lasting impression, making it the centerpiece of any event.
    2. Storytelling Through Design
    - Decorations can reflect a theme, color scheme, or even a personal story, adding a unique touch to the occasion.
    3. Professionalism
    - Advanced techniques signal skill and care, elevating your cakes from homemade to professional quality.

Essential Tools for Advanced Cake Decorating

1. Piping Tools
    - Piping Bags: Use reusable or disposable bags for applying frosting.
    - Piping Tips: Tips like round, star, and petal are essential for creating various designs.
    - Couplers: Allow you to switch tips without changing bags.
    2. Fondant Tools

- Fondant Smoothers: Help achieve a polished finish.

- Cutters and Molds: Create shapes, patterns, and decorations.

- Edible Paints and Brushes: Add fine details or metallic accents.

3. Sugar Flower Tools

- Petal Cutters: Shape sugar paste into petals and leaves.

- Veining Tools: Add realistic textures.

- Wire and Floral Tape: Assemble flowers securely.

4. Tiered Cake Assembly

- Cake Boards: Provide stability for each tier.

- Dowels or Straws: Support the weight of upper tiers.

- Offset Spatula: Smooth frosting layers.

Advanced Piping Techniques

Piping is one of the most versatile and visually impactful decorating methods. With practice and the right tools, you can create intricate designs, elegant borders, and lifelike flowers.

1. Mastering Piping Consistency

- Ensure your frosting is the right consistency: firm enough to hold shape but soft enough to pipe smoothly.

- For intricate designs, use royal icing for its stability.

2. Popular Piping Techniques

- Rosettes: Use a star tip to pipe spiral rosettes for a classic design.

- Basketweave: Create a woven texture using a flat piping tip.

- Shell Borders: Add a polished finish to the base or edges of a cake using a star tip.

- Lacework: Use a small round tip to pipe delicate patterns resembling lace.

3. Practice Makes Perfect

- Use a practice board or parchment paper to refine your piping skills before decorating the actual cake.

- Maintain steady pressure on the piping bag for consistent designs.

Working with Fondant

Fondant provides a smooth, flawless canvas for decorating and can be shaped into intricate designs, making it indispensable for professional-quality cakes.

1. Preparing Fondant

- Knead fondant until pliable before rolling it out.

- Dust your work surface with cornstarch or powdered sugar to prevent sticking.

2. Covering a Cake with Fondant

1. Roll the fondant to about 1/8-inch thickness.

2. Drape it over a crumb-coated cake and smooth it with your hands and fondant smoothers.

3. Trim excess fondant at the base using a sharp knife or pizza cutter.

3. Creating Fondant Decorations

- Cut-Out Shapes: Use cutters to make stars, hearts, or other designs.

- Embossing and Stenciling: Add patterns using embossing mats or stencils.

- Sculpting: Shape fondant into figures, flowers, or bows.

4. Painting on Fondant

- Use edible food coloring or metallic paints to add fine details or accents.

- Thin gel food coloring with vodka or lemon extract for a watercolor effect.

Crafting Sugar Flowers

Sugar flowers are delicate and lifelike decorations that add elegance to cakes, especially for weddings and special events.

1. Preparing Sugar Paste (Gum Paste)

- Use gum paste for sugar flowers as it dries hard and holds intricate shapes.

- Knead the paste until smooth and pliable before rolling it thin.

2. Basic Sugar Flower Steps

1. Cut Petals: Use petal cutters to create individual flower components.

2. Add Texture: Use veining tools or silicone molds to add realistic details.

3. Shape Petals: Use a ball tool to thin and curl the edges for a natural look.

4. Assemble the Flower: Attach petals to a wire stem using edible glue. Wrap the stem with floral tape.

3. Popular Sugar Flowers

- Roses: Classic and versatile, suitable for any occasion.
- Peonies: Full and ruffled, ideal for romantic designs.
- Orchids: Elegant and exotic, perfect for modern cakes.
4. Coloring Sugar Flowers
- Use petal dusts to add subtle shading and depth.
- Steam the flowers briefly to set the colors and give a natural sheen.

Building Layered and Tiered Cakes

Layered and tiered cakes require structural integrity and attention to detail to achieve a stunning presentation.

1. Preparing Layers
- Trim cake layers to ensure they are even.
- Use a cake leveler or serrated knife for precision.
- Apply a thin crumb coat to seal in crumbs and create a smooth base for frosting or fondant.

2. Assembling Tiered Cakes
1. Place the bottom tier on a sturdy cake board.
2. Insert dowels or straws into the bottom tier for support. Trim them to the height of the cake.
3. Place the next tier on its own cake board and position it on top of the dowels. Repeat for additional tiers.
4. Decorate each tier individually or after assembly, depending on the design.

3. Transporting Tiered Cakes
- Chill the cake thoroughly before transport to ensure stability.
- Use a sturdy box or cake carrier for safe handling.

Decorating for Weddings and Special Events

1. Color Palettes and Themes
- Coordinate cake colors with the event's theme or decor.
- Use soft pastels for romantic events and bold colors for modern celebrations.
2. Edible Accents

- Incorporate gold leaf, edible pearls, or lace-like royal icing details for elegance.

- Use fresh flowers, ensuring they are food-safe and pesticide-free.

3. Personalization

- Add monograms, names, or meaningful motifs to make the cake unique to the event.

Common Challenges and Solutions

1. Fondant Tears

- Patch small tears with a bit of water and smooth with your fingers or a fondant smoother.

2. Uneven Layers

- Use a cake leveler or serrated knife to trim layers before stacking.

3. Melting Decorations

- Store cakes with delicate decorations in a cool, dry place. Avoid humidity, which can cause fondant or sugar flowers to soften.

Conclusion

Advanced decorating techniques transform cakes into edible works of art, perfect for weddings, birthdays, and other memorable events. From mastering intricate piping and working with fondant to crafting lifelike sugar flowers and building tiered cakes, this chapter provides the skills and inspiration to create professional-quality cakes. With practice, patience, and creativity, you can bring your most ambitious cake designs to life, making each creation a masterpiece that delights both the eyes and the taste buds. Let this chapter inspire you to push the boundaries of your baking artistry and create stunning cakes for every occasion.

Chapter 15: Troubleshooting and Variations

Baking cakes is both an art and a science, and even the most experienced bakers encounter challenges in the kitchen. From sunken centers to crumbly textures, cake-baking problems are common but solvable. Equally important is the ability to adapt recipes to suit your tastes or dietary needs, allowing you to create unique variations and elevate your baking. This chapter is a comprehensive guide to troubleshooting common issues and exploring creative ways to adapt cake recipes.

The Science of Cake Baking

Before diving into troubleshooting, it's helpful to understand the basic elements of cake baking. Cakes rely on a delicate balance of ingredients, temperature, and technique. Each ingredient plays a specific role:

1. Flour: Provides structure through gluten or alternative proteins in gluten-free baking.

2. Sugar: Adds sweetness and tenderizes the crumb.

3. Fats (butter, oil): Contribute to moisture, richness, and flavor.

4. Leavening Agents (baking powder, baking soda): Help the cake rise.

5. Eggs: Bind ingredients, provide structure, and add moisture.

6. Liquids (milk, buttermilk): Hydrate dry ingredients and contribute to texture.

When these elements are imbalanced or mishandled, problems arise.

Common Cake-Baking Problems and Solutions

1. Sunken Cake Centers
- Cause: Overmixing, underbaking, or too much leavening.
- Solution:
- Mix batter just until combined to avoid incorporating excess air.
- Use the correct amount of leavening agent.
- Test for doneness with a toothpick before removing the cake from the oven.
2. Dry or Crumbly Cake

- Cause: Overbaking, too much flour, or not enough fat or liquid.

- Solution:

- Measure flour accurately by spooning it into the measuring cup and leveling it off.

- Reduce baking time or temperature slightly.

- Incorporate ingredients like yogurt, sour cream, or applesauce for added moisture.

3. Dense Texture

- Cause: Overmixing, incorrect leavening, or too little leavening.

- Solution:

- Mix batter gently, especially after adding flour.

- Ensure baking powder or soda is fresh.

- Follow recipe instructions for proper leavening ratios.

4. Uneven Layers

- Cause: Uneven oven temperature or improperly leveled batter.

- Solution:

- Rotate pans halfway through baking for even heat distribution.

- Use a kitchen scale to divide batter evenly between pans.

5. Cracked Tops

- Cause: Oven temperature too high or overfilled pans.

- Solution:

- Lower the oven temperature by 25°F (15°C).

- Fill pans only two-thirds full.

6. Sticky or Gummy Texture

- Cause: Underbaking or too much sugar or liquid.

- Solution:

- Bake until a toothpick inserted in the center comes out clean.

- Reduce sugar slightly if the recipe is overly sweet.

7. Cake Sticks to the Pan

- Cause: Insufficient greasing or improper cooling.

- Solution:

- Grease pans thoroughly with butter or nonstick spray and line with parchment paper.

- Cool cakes for 10–15 minutes before removing from the pan.

8. Frosting Issues

- Too Runny: Add powdered sugar or chill the frosting briefly.

- Too Thick: Add a splash of milk or cream to thin.

- Separating: Beat on low speed until smooth.

Creative Variations and Flavor Adaptations

1. Infusing Flavors

- Spices: Add cinnamon, cardamom, nutmeg, or ginger for warmth.

- Citrus Zest: Incorporate lemon, lime, or orange zest for brightness.

- Extracts: Swap vanilla for almond, coconut, or rose water for a unique twist.

2. Mixing Textures

- Add-ins: Stir in nuts, chocolate chips, dried fruit, or shredded coconut.

- Fillings: Use jams, curds, ganache, or fruit compotes between layers.

3. Experimenting with Flours

- Use almond or coconut flour for gluten-free options.

- Replace part of the all-purpose flour with whole wheat or spelt for a nuttier flavor.

4. Playing with Sweeteners

- Replace refined sugar with honey, maple syrup, coconut sugar, or agave.

- Reduce sugar and compensate with naturally sweet ingredients like mashed bananas or applesauce.

5. Incorporating Liquids

- Substitute milk with buttermilk, yogurt, or plant-based alternatives for different textures and flavors.

- Add coffee, tea, or liqueurs for depth.

6. Adapting for Dietary Needs

- Egg-Free: Use flaxseed or chia seed eggs, applesauce, or mashed bananas as substitutes.

- Dairy-Free: Replace butter with coconut oil or vegan butter; use almond or oat milk instead of dairy milk.

- Gluten-Free: Blend gluten-free all-purpose flour with almond flour for better structure.

Examples of Recipe Variations

1. Chocolate Cake Variations
    - Add espresso powder for a mocha twist.
    - Stir in chili powder or cayenne for a Mexican hot chocolate flavor.
    - Use orange zest and Grand Marnier for a citrusy spin.
    2. Vanilla Cake Variations
    - Infuse with lavender or earl grey tea for floral notes.
    - Add crushed freeze-dried strawberries for a fruity flavor.
    - Mix in shredded coconut and lime zest for a tropical feel.
    3. Carrot Cake Variations
    - Substitute pineapple for raisins to add moisture.
    - Add chopped pecans or walnuts for crunch.
    - Use a cream cheese frosting infused with maple syrup or orange zest.
    4. Cheesecake Variations
    - Swirl in fruit puree or jam for a marbled effect.
    - Add a layer of ganache for a decadent topping.
    - Use crushed ginger snaps instead of graham crackers for the crust.

Encouragement to Experiment

1. Start with a Base Recipe
    - Use a reliable base recipe as a foundation and make small changes, like swapping one ingredient or adjusting flavorings.
    2. Keep a Baking Journal
    - Record your experiments, noting changes, successes, and areas for improvement.
    3. Taste as You Go
    - Sample batter, fillings, and frosting to ensure the flavors are balanced.
    4. Embrace Mistakes
    - View baking mishaps as opportunities to learn and refine your technique.
    - Repurpose failed cakes into trifles, cake pops, or crumb toppings.
    5. Share Your Creations

- Involve friends or family in tasting and give them input on new variations.

Examples of Unique Creations

1. Lemon Thyme Cake
    - Add lemon zest and fresh thyme to the batter. Pair with a honey glaze.
    2. Matcha and Black Sesame Cake
- Infuse the batter with matcha powder and swirl black sesame paste into the layers.
    3. Spiced Chai Cake
- Mix ground chai spices into the batter and top with cream cheese frosting infused with vanilla and cardamom.
    4. S'mores Cake
- Use a graham cracker crust, chocolate cake layers, and toasted marshmallow frosting.

Conclusion

Baking is a dynamic process, and every challenge or variation is an opportunity to grow as a baker. By understanding the science behind common cake problems and exploring creative adaptations, you can transform setbacks into successes and simple recipes into extraordinary desserts. This chapter encourages you to experiment fearlessly, make each recipe your own, and enjoy the journey of baking. Remember, every cake tells a story—let yours be one of creativity, resilience, and delicious innovation.

Conclusion

Baking a cake is more than just a culinary task; it's an act of creativity, love, and celebration. From the simple joy of mixing batter to the final reveal of a beautifully decorated masterpiece, baking embodies the spirit of sharing and connection. Cakes have been at the heart of our celebrations for centuries, marking birthdays, weddings, holidays, and milestones with their sweetness and charm.

As this book concludes, we take a moment to reflect on the journey of cake baking, celebrate its joys, and provide final tips and resources to encourage you to keep exploring and experimenting in the kitchen.

The Joy of Baking Cakes

1. A Universal Language

Cakes transcend borders, cultures, and occasions. A slice of cake speaks of comfort, happiness, and generosity. Whether it's a rich chocolate cake for a birthday, a delicate opera cake for an anniversary, or a simple loaf cake shared over coffee, cakes bring people together.

2. A Creative Outlet

Baking offers endless possibilities for artistic expression. From crafting intricate sugar flowers to experimenting with flavors and textures, each cake is an opportunity to showcase your unique style and personality.

3. A Symbol of Celebration

Cakes are synonymous with celebration. They symbolize joy, gratitude, and togetherness. The act of baking, sharing, and enjoying a cake embodies the essence of life's sweetest moments.

Final Tips for Aspiring Bakers

1. Master the Basics

- Building a strong foundation in cake baking is key. Focus on mastering basic recipes, techniques, and tools before venturing into advanced methods.

- Perfect foundational recipes like a simple sponge cake, a reliable buttercream, and a classic chocolate cake.

2. Embrace Challenges

- Mistakes are an inevitable part of baking, especially when experimenting with new techniques. Use these challenges as opportunities to learn and improve.

- Keep a baking journal to note successes, adjustments, and areas for growth.

3. Experiment with Flavors

- Don't be afraid to try unconventional combinations or adapt recipes to incorporate your favorite ingredients.

- Explore seasonal produce, unique spices, and international influences to expand your repertoire.

4. Prioritize Quality Ingredients

- Using high-quality ingredients—like fresh eggs, premium chocolate, and pure vanilla extract—can elevate even the simplest cakes.

- Support local markets and specialty stores for unique and fresh ingredients.

5. Pay Attention to Details

- Precision is critical in baking. Measure ingredients accurately, follow instructions closely, and pay attention to baking times and temperatures.

- Focus on presentation, as visual appeal enhances the overall experience of a cake.

Encouragement to Explore and Experiment

1. Break Free from Recipes

- Once you've mastered the basics, let your creativity shine by altering recipes, adding unique twists, or designing your own cakes from scratch.

2. Incorporate Personal Stories

- Create cakes that reflect your personal history, culture, or memories. For example, recreate a cake from your childhood or design one inspired by your travels.

3. Collaborate and Share

- Baking can be a collaborative effort. Involve family, friends, or even children in the process, turning it into a bonding activity.

- Share your creations with others to spread joy and receive feedback.

4. Take Inspiration from Others

- Follow professional bakers, watch tutorials, and explore baking books or blogs for fresh ideas.

- Attend workshops or classes to refine your skills and learn new techniques.

5. Enjoy the Process

- Baking is as much about the journey as it is about the finished product. Enjoy each step, from measuring ingredients to decorating the final masterpiece.

Resources for Further Learning and Inspiration

Books and Magazines

- Invest in reputable baking books, from beginner guides to advanced techniques.

- Subscribe to baking magazines for seasonal recipes, trends, and expert tips.

Online Resources

- Explore baking blogs, YouTube channels, and social media platforms for tutorials and inspiration.

- Join online baking communities or forums to connect with fellow enthusiasts.

Workshops and Classes

- Enroll in local or online baking classes to learn from professionals and gain hands-on experience.

- Attend baking expos or demonstrations to discover new tools, ingredients, and methods.

Ingredients and Tools

- Visit specialty stores for unique ingredients, like edible flowers, gourmet spices, or artisanal chocolates.

- Upgrade your baking tools, such as stand mixers, high-quality pans, or precision thermometers, to enhance your craft.

Reflecting on the Journey

1. Milestones in Baking

Think back to your first attempt at baking a cake and compare it to where you are now. Celebrate the progress you've made, from mastering simple recipes to tackling complex designs.

2. Moments of Joy

Recall the smiles and compliments your cakes have brought to others. Each cake is a gift, and the joy it spreads is a testament to your skill and effort.

3. Looking Ahead

There's always more to learn in the world of baking. Whether it's exploring global cake traditions, perfecting advanced techniques, or inventing new recipes, the possibilities are endless.

Closing Thoughts

As you close this book, remember that every cake you bake is a reflection of your passion, creativity, and dedication. Whether you're baking for a special occasion, experimenting with new flavors, or simply enjoying the process, each cake is an opportunity to bring happiness to yourself and others.

Keep experimenting, keep learning, and, most importantly, keep baking. The world of cakes is vast, and your journey has only just begun. Celebrate the art of baking, savor the sweetness of success, and share your creations with the world.

Happy baking!

Don't miss out!

Visit the website below and you can sign up to receive emails whenever Olivia Bennett publishes a new book. There's no charge and no obligation.

https://books2read.com/r/B-A-QLEKD-MMQAG

BOOKS2READ

Connecting independent readers to independent writers.

About the Author

Olivia Bennett is a celebrated food writer and chef with expertise spanning multiple culinary disciplines. With a passion for making home cooking accessible, she specializes in guiding readers through everything from hearty casseroles to delicate pastries. Her work is known for its clear instructions, practical tips, and deep understanding of both traditional and modern cooking techniques.